SONG
of SONGS

The Song of Solomon is one of the most abused, misused, and misunderstood books in the history of biblical interpretation. Sound, theologically orthodox, and exegetically rich commentaries on Solomon's Song are rare. This commentary, however, is all of those things and more. Jim Hamilton has produced a fresh, biblically-theologically informed approach to the Song of Solomon. This is a commentary pastors should regularly turn to when preaching through this important but difficult book of Scripture. And make no mistake—reading this commentary will make you want to preach this book.

R. Albert Mohler,
President,
The Southern Baptist Theological Seminary, Louisville, Kentucky

This beautifully written book of sound Christ-centered biblical exposition and skillful personal application, will not only strengthen and heal many marriages, but will also draw many Christians into a deeper appreciation and enjoyment of their marriage to Christ. Unlike most books on the Song of Songs, this one will make you sing!

David Murray,
Professor of Old Testament & Practical Theology,
Puritan Reformed Theological Seminary, Grand Rapids, Michigan

SONG
of SONGS

A Biblical-Theological, Allegorical,
Christological Interpretation

James M. Hamilton Jr.

James M. Hamilton Jr. serves as Professor of Biblical Theology at Southern Seminary and as Preaching Pastor at Kenwood Baptist Church, Louisville, Kentucky. He is married with five children.

Copyright © 2015 James M. Hamilton Jr.

ISBN 978-1-78191-560-8

10 9 8 7 6 5 4 3 2 1

Printed in 2015
by
Christian Focus Publications Ltd.,
Geanies House, Fearn, Ross-shire,
IV20 1TW, Scotland, U.K.

www.christianfocus.com

Cover design by Daniel van Straaten

Printed and bound by
Bell & Bain, Glasgow

MIX
Paper from
responsible sources
FSC
www.fsc.org FSC® C007785

Contents

for Jillian Ashley Hamilton
as one from two we enjoy
the music of this the
most sublime
Song

Preface

The Song of Songs is one of my favorite books in the Bible. I was barely aware it existed when my dear friend Kameron Slater introduced me to Tommy Nelson's sermon series on the book in my sophomore year at the University of Arkansas. I listened to the cassette tapes of those sermons over and over, invested much time meditating on the Song, and memorized wide swaths of the poetry.

I don't remember being taught to read the book as a member of the bride of Christ waiting for Jesus the bridegroom. As a Christian, that came naturally. I do remember being taught — at least some teachers tried to convince me — that the book was *only* about human love with no reference to the relationship between God and His people. Looking back I think the best efforts of those well-meaning teachers knocked me off balance, left me not quite sure what to do with the book. Then I heard John Sailhamer say that the whole of the Old Testament was written to provoke and sustain a messianic hope,[1] an idea that immediately took hold in my thinking. I applied the idea to the Song of Songs, confident that the book was advancing the fulfillment of the blessing of Abraham through the Davidic Messiah, but at that time I wanted to avoid any suggestion of allegory.[2]

The kind of allegory I wanted to avoid was the kind practiced by Philo and Origen, and at that time I was not in a position to distinguish their brand of allegory from what Paul

---

1. John Sailhamer, 'The Messiah and the Hebrew Bible,' *Journal of the Evangelical Theological Society* 44 (2001): 5-23.

2. James M. Hamilton Jr., 'The Messianic Music of the Song of Songs: A Non-Allegorical Interpretation,' *Westminster Theological Journal* 68 (2006): 331-45.

does in Galatians 4:21-31. To be quite honest, the fact that Paul said 'Now this may be interpreted allegorically' (Gal. 4:24) made me really nervous.

Continued study of the Scriptures has led me to the position that the task of biblical theology is one of learning to understand and embrace the interpretive perspective of the biblical authors.[3] Gradually I came to the view that if Moses can treat the covenant between Yahweh and Israel as a marriage, and if Hosea can write a prophecy in which he himself represents Yahweh and his wife Gomer represents Israel, Solomon could have done the same. Approaching the Song of Songs from this perspective fits perfectly with what Paul says marriage means in Ephesians 5, and I have tried to explain the Song of Songs and its glorious detail from this perspective. I do not deny that the Song is about human love. I contend that Solomon intended his audience to detect a correspondence between the King's marriage to his Bride and Yahweh's covenant with Israel.

What words could communicate my gratitude for the Song of Songs? How could letters on a page combine to tell of the joy that comes from living in accordance with God's instructions? Blessed be the name of the Lord. His mercy endures forever. I thank God by the power of the Spirit in the name of Jesus for saving me, for granting me the opportunity to serve Him and His people, and for the privilege of studying and teaching the Bible.

This book grew out of the nine sermons I preached on the Song of Songs at Kenwood Baptist Church in Louisville, Kentucky, beginning on 19 August and continuing until 21 October, 2012. God our Father has been so good to us at Kenwood, graciously answering Jesus' prayer for us to be sanctified by the truth of His Word (John 17:17).

I am thankful that Willie MacKenzie invited me to write this book, as terrified as I was to undertake the task. As I began to pray and study, God met me in His Word in mercy and grace beyond what tongue can tell.

If I could wield the words of Shakespeare, I might begin to say how grateful I am for my sweet wife. If words could plumb the depths of human emotion, I could perhaps employ

---

3. See my book, *What Is Biblical Theology?* (Wheaton: Crossway, 2014).

them to write what she means to me. Alas, my faltering and feeble faculties can only do the best they can: this book is for my sweet Jill. I dedicate it to her with all my heart. She is the lady with whom I am privileged to live out the lyrical love of this most sublime Song, the mother of my children, the joy of my days, the bride of my youth. I exult that she said yes, that she took on my name.

Thank you, my love, for giving your life to me.

James M. Hamilton Jr.
17 February, 2014

I

The Song of Songs in Biblical Theology: How to Read the Most Sublime Song

Why is the Song of Songs in the Bible, and how are we to understand it? This Song's music calls us to a better life, and we hear the music through God's life-changing Word.

The Song of Songs, which is Solomon's, sings us right into reality. The mesmerizing Song captivates our attention, wooing our hearts and winning our minds, demonstrating that the way of life depicted in its poetry is more real than the world's version of the good life.

The Bible's overarching story is bigger and grander and higher and deeper and longer and wider and more significant than any other narrative human tongues can tell. The Bible's truth is solid, clear, and forceful, like a faithful foundation when philosophies fail, the house built on it tall and true when falsehoods fall.

Behold, too, the emotional range of the book: the statements of pain in Scripture plumb as deep as any suffer, and the Bible's depiction of love, particularly in the Song of Songs, shines brighter even than Shakespeare's lyric glory. The Song sings what we would long for in our hearts if we knew how to hope for heaven.

The Bible's presentation of life as it should be is better than life as we usually experience it. There are moments when we feel the love for God that we should, the power of His truth that we should, the love for the church and the lost that we should, and the love for our spouses or the devotion to marriage that we should, but the Bible is constant. The Bible shows the way to a life more authentic, more appropriate, more true, more sorrowful, more joyful, and more loving than what mere fallen flesh could find for itself. The Bible is more real than the world, and the sublime music of the Song of Songs sings it is so.

The people of God need the Word of God, and we desperately need the Song of Songs today. Our time is notable for massive sexual confusion, distortion, and perversion. Pornography is pervasive. Adultery is celebrated in the culture at large, the devastation of divorce normalized, the fiction of same-sex marriage legalized—all satanic attempts to make immorality moral through the permission of the legislature. In this subverted moral universe, those who adhere to morality as the Bible asserts the Creator intended it are regarded as bigots, or worse.

As a result of the Fall, we who are Christians experience deeply distorted and destructive instincts and attitudes about sexuality. Even among the redeemed we can find broken and damaged marriages. Some members of the bride of Christ harbor unrealistic expectations about what marriage will be like, about what our needs are, and about how to achieve satisfaction.

How are we to straighten out our crooked thinking, find healing for old wounds, and be renewed in our minds when it comes to marriage and sex? God's Word is living and active. God's Word is relevant. God's Word is able to make us wise unto salvation. And I am confident that God has given us the Song of Solomon so that we will think rightly about sexuality. As we present the living sacrifices of our lives—even in our sexuality—to the One who showed us mercy (Rom. 12:1-2), the Song of Songs is one of the tools the Spirit of God will use to conform us to the image of Christ, to transform us from one degree of glory to another, to enable us to take every thought captive to the knowledge of Christ.

God has given us the Song of Solomon so that His glory in Christ will shine in our marriages and in our sexuality. We want the glory of God in Christ to shine in the way we think about and live out the emotional and physical intimacy God intends for husbands and wives by the power of the Spirit.

The Song of Songs is inviting, exciting, and daunting, and God will use it to make us love Him, to make us long for Christ, and to make us better single people and better spouses, better adolescents and better adults, better children and better parents. The Bible is more real than the world, and the way to live in the Bible's account of reality, which *is* the real world, is to steep ourselves in it, to understand it, to relish it, meditating on it day and night.

This first chapter is on how to read and think about the Song of Songs. So I ask again: what is the Song of Solomon doing in the Bible, and how are we to understand it?[1]

What is the Song of Songs?

Is this short book of poetry an allegory that has nothing to do with human love and everything to do with Yahweh and Israel or Christ and the church? Or is it to be read as though it is *only* dealing with the love between a man and a woman? Could it be *both* about God and Israel, Christ and the church, *and also* about love between a man and woman in marriage?

Is Solomon's a narrative Song, one that begins with betrothal, proceeds to marriage, moves on to the deepening intimacy of that marriage, ending with reflections on love?[2] Did Solomon intend this book to be an instruction manual for couples to increase their enjoyment of physical aspects of marital intimacy?

Does this book have anything to do with the Bible's big story, with earlier Old Testament narratives, prophecies, patterns, and promises? How are we to navigate these questions and find answers to them?

---

1. For a very detailed history of interpretation, see Marvin H. Pope, *Song of Songs*, Anchor Bible (Garden City, N.Y.: Doubleday, 1977), 89-229; see also the very important book by Gerald Bray, *Biblical Interpretation: Past and Present* (Downers Grove: InterVarsity, 1996), particularly his case study on the Song of Songs, 159-64; and the most detailed and comprehensive analysis of virtually everything pertaining to the Song is the 1,300-page tome by Christopher W. Mitchell, *The Song of Songs*, Concordia Commentary (St. Louis: Concordia, 2003).

2. So Daniel J. Estes in Daniel C. Fredericks and Daniel J. Estes, *Ecclesiastes and the Song of Songs*, Apollos Old Testament Commentary (Downers Grove: InterVarsity, 2010), 292.

How Should We Read It?

The main point of this first chapter is that the *Song* of Solomon should be read as *what* it is *where* it is. That is to say, this book is a *Song* and it's *in the Bible*. Those may seem to be simple assertions, but my aim is to explain how those two assertions affect everything about how we understand this book. So I say again: the Song of Songs should be read as *what* it is *where* it is, a *Song* that is *in the Bible*. Let me explain.

First, this book is a Song: it's one poem. The first word of the book's title is in the singular: the *Song* of Songs. So we are *not* dealing with a collection of smaller songs. This book is not an anthology of short poems but *one unified piece of poetry*, and it should therefore be interpreted as a unit, as a whole. So the Song is *one poem*, not a collection of several poems, and the fact that it is a song means that its author *intended* it to be poetic and therefore evocative.

Other forms of writing (genres) are used when authors intend to be precise, technical, and specific, but when authors write poetry the use of language tends to suggest multiple interpretations, sometimes even multiple layers of interpretation. We must let the genre—the fact that we are reading *poetry*—inform how we read this book: we should not close down the possible meanings a poem awakens but explore them. This does not mean every possible meaning will have equal value. We should pursue the meaning(s) intended by the author, which leads from *what* this book is to *where* it is.

Second, this Song is in the Bible. That means that we should read the Song in light of the bigger story that is unfolding in the whole Bible. We should read the Song as summarizing and interpreting the big story of the Bible, contributing to it, depicting it in verse.[3]

This means that the Song of Songs sings the Bible's love story. Reflecting on these realities will help us tune our ears so that we can listen more closely to the Song. In the rest of this chapter we consider the broader story being summarized and interpreted in the Song before we give it a close listen. We

---

3. For a large-scale look at the Bible's big story, see James M. Hamilton Jr., *God's Glory in Salvation through Judgment: A Biblical Theology* (Wheaton: Crossway, 2010), and for a shorter version, with some attention to the way the Bible's imagery and symbolism summarizes and interprets the big story, see Hamilton, *What Is Biblical Theology?*.

want to know more effectively how to deal with the imagery that will be used, so that it might be less befuddling and more inspiring when we encounter it.

To that end, we will consider the setting, plot, hero, and meaning of the Song. The four parts are as follows:

The Song's Setting: Thorns and Thistles, Rivered Garden

The Song's Plot: Garments of Skin, Exposed and Unashamed

The Song's Hero: David's Son, the new Adam

The Song's Meaning: Poetry, Allegory, Typology, Oh My!

Before plunging forward, however, a word is in order about the music other books of the Bible make. We should think of the Song of Solomon as one movement in the grand symphonic poem of the Bible. It's a beautiful movement. Its title claims it is the most sublime Song, but it's not the only music in the Bible that deals with these themes.

The Song of Songs has music of intimacy and fervor, and there are other parts of the Bible that depict other things we need to know about love and marriage. For instance, near the Song, the book of Ecclesiastes balances the message of the Song by telling us there is a time for everything (Eccles. 3:1-8), and that in all things we must fear God and keep His commandments (12:13-14). In Proverbs 5:15-23, husbands are warned against seeking marital delights outside of marriage (cf. also Prov. 7, etc.). As the exemplary father in Proverbs addresses his instruction to his son (cf. 'My son ...' in Prov. 2:1; 3:1, etc.), we see a husband who has become a father who is obeying the instructions in Deuteronomy 6:7 for fathers to teach their sons diligently.[4] And then Proverbs 31 presents us with an exemplary wife and mother doing many things to bless her husband and children.[5]

The Bible speaks to all aspects of what it means to be a husband or a wife, a father or mother. There are parts of the Bible that sing a song of singleness (e.g., Matt. 19:11-12; 1 Cor. 7:7, 32). So if you're not at an age to be married yet, or

---

4. On this, see further James M. Hamilton Jr., 'That the Coming Generation Might Praise the Lord,' *Journal of Family Ministry* 1 (2010): 10-17.

5. On which, see James M. Hamilton Jr., 'A Biblical Theology of Motherhood,' *Journal of Discipleship and Family Ministry* 2, no. 2 (2012): 6-13.

if you're at the age and unmarried, or if you're a widow or a widower, or if for whatever reason you're inclined to think that maybe this book isn't singing your song, let me encourage you to lend your ear anyway. I know that other parts of the music might be more directly relevant to where you are at the moment, but I'm confident that listening to this part of the music will only make the rest of it better.

All Scripture is 'breathed out by God and profitable,' and it will all be used to 'complete' and equip us (2 Tim. 3:16; Eph. 4:11-16); it's all written for our instruction to give us hope (Rom. 15:4), and the Lord will use this part of His Word to help us long for Christ and enable us to feel the meaning of Revelation 22:17, where 'the Spirit and the Bride say, "Come."And let the one who hears say, "Come." And let the one who is thirsty come; let the one who desires take the water of life without price.' And we'll join John in the words of Revelation 22:20, 'Amen. Come, Lord Jesus!'

We begin with the physical setting of the Song.

The Song's Setting: Thorns and Thistles, Rivered Garden

The setting of the Song of Songs is remarkably reminiscent of Eden,[6] where all the women really would have been strong, the men good-looking, and all the children above average. There once really was a Camelot, but the iconic innocence of the place wasn't in an England ruled by an Arthur. No, it was a place where everything was very good. No Lancelot lurked to lead Guinevere astray, though came a day when a serpent scorned the Word of God, tempted the woman, and man fell into sin. Before we get to sin, though, meditate for a moment on the very good land that was.

Think back through the curses of Genesis 3:14-19, starting with the last first: can you imagine an *uncursed* land? I think

---

6. I am convinced that Solomon, the author of the Song, intended to evoke Eden, so I disagree with Garrett's suggestion that 'Relating the Song to Genesis 2—3 is ... extraneous,' that the 'ties [to Gen. 1—3] are of dubious value,' and that 'when an interpreter repeatedly turns to Genesis to find the meaning of the Song, it is obvious that the alleged meaning is not germane to the Song at all,' in Duane A. Garrett and Paul R. House, *Song of Songs, Lamentations*, Word Biblical Commentary (Nashville: Thomas Nelson, 2004), 99. If we approach the text from the perspective that Solomon was a biblical theologian whose view of the world was shaped by earlier Scripture, it is natural to read the text in its canonical context, summarizing and interpreting the broader biblical story.

you can. It's what you picture being beyond the rainbow, or it's what we wish we could find when we finally arrive. We have this longing for something better than we currently experience, and we feel a desire for everything to be just right. C. S. Lewis wrote, 'If I find in myself a desire which nothing in this world can satisfy, the only logical explanation is that I was made for another world.'[7] The world was another kind of place before sin, one that had no curse, where all was very good (cf. Gen. 3:17-19).

Can you imagine a world where men and women got along perfectly, never a hitch in their interactions? Can you imagine a world where women did not die in childbirth, where babies always came out of the womb alive and healthy, indeed, a world where childbirth was not painful? Every time there's a death in childbirth, we should respond: this is not the way it's supposed to be. That response is right because when God made the world, there was no sin or death, there was no conflict between men and women, and there was no pain in childbearing (cf. Gen. 3:16).

Can you imagine a world with no evil and no enemies? I'm not talking about moral relativism that denies that anything is evil. I'm talking about a world where everyone would always choose what is true and good, a world where everyone really would be reasonable, and we really could talk through differences. If you haven't noticed, that's not the world in which we live. We all think the world should be that way, don't we? We all wish that nations could have good-faith agreements and treaties that everyone could agree to as good and right so that all war could be avoided, all weapons unmade, and all peace enjoyed. When God made the world, there was no enmity between people groups; there was no curse on the serpent and his seed (cf. Gen. 3:15).

Prior to Genesis 3:14-19, where God cursed the serpent and his seed, caused the woman to desire to control her husband, added pain in childbearing, and cursed the land, making toil painful, the world was as it was meant to be: 'very good' (Gen. 1:31). The land was well watered and un-cursed. There

---

7. C. S. Lewis, *Mere Christianity* (San Francisco: HarperCollins, 1996), 136-7.

were no enemies full of enmity. And the man and his wife were naked and unashamed (2:25).

Sin had not yet entered the world through one man, and death through sin (Rom. 5:12). After sin, God spoke judgment, and Adam and Eve were driven from the garden God had planted in Eden in the east (Gen. 2:8; 3:22-24).

The closest we get to being back to the Garden of Eden in the rest of the Bible is in the poetry of the Song of Songs.

Do you want to read of the fruits and foliage of Eden? Read the Song of Songs. Do you want to know what it would have been like for Adam and Eve to gaze on one another in their native majesty, unarrayed by clothing, feeling neither shame nor fear? Read the Song of Songs. Do you want to see man and wife moving past hostility and alienation into harmony and oneness? Read the Song of Songs.

The Song is set in basically two places, and the two complement one another. On the one hand, there is a garden setting, and this garden looks cultivated. It looks like it has a new-Adam kind of figure who works and keeps it, which was what God put Adam in the garden to do. The Song of Songs shows us a fertile land yielding its fruit to the hand of a gardener wise and good.

On the other hand, the Song is set in Zion, Jerusalem, the city of David. There is a trajectory in the Old Testament from the Garden of Eden to the Tabernacle to the Temple, with Jerusalem, the capital of the land, being a kind of focal point of the new Eden that the land of promise represents. This means that these two settings are not that different from one another. Just as there is a direct line from Adam to David, there is a direct line from Eden to Zion. This trajectory, this thematic line from Eden to Zion, points forward to the new heaven and new earth, which is itself a new temple and a new Eden.[8]

As we read the Song of Solomon, then, the setting of this song that summarizes and interprets the Bible's big story should call to our minds the way that the story began in God's very good creation, the undefiled garden in Eden in the east. Man was driven from Eden because of sin, the land was cursed, the creation subjected to futility ... in hope

---

8. On this theme, see G. K. Beale, *The Temple and the Church's Mission: A Biblical Theology of the Dwelling Place of God* (Downers Grove: InterVarsity, 2004).

(Rom. 8:20), and those hopes are evoked in this Song, as the one who descends from Adam, the seed of the woman, has cultivated a garden-city that is not only habitable but lush and is causing the blessing of Abraham, the blessing of the land, to be enjoyed by all who benefit from the way he works and keeps the garden-city.

The Song of Songs is a song of hope. A hope not vague but specific: that one day the curse will be rolled back, the land will have no more famines, and all will again be very good under the hand of the one who works and keeps the garden. The Song of Songs does not portray the new heaven and earth directly, but its setting is reminiscent of the fertility of Eden, thereby pointing forward to a new and better Eden.

The Song's Plot: Garments of Skin, Exposed and Unashamed

We have been considering how the situation in Genesis 1:31, where 'God saw everything that he had made, and behold, it was very good,' came to an end when 'the creation was subjected to futility … in hope' (Rom. 8:20). We turn our attention now to consider a beauty that deserves the reverence of the holy of holies. Solomon was no doubt aware of the correspondence between the phrases 'Song of Songs' and 'Holy of Holies.' The holiness of the holy place in both tabernacle and temple was reminiscent of Eden, and these most holy places were meant to create sacred space where God would be present. The presence of God is a significant consideration as we consider nakedness and clothing and intimacy.

The Book of Kings presents Solomon as a man who knew plants and built the temple (1 Kings 4:33; 6:37-38). He exercised dominion over the land and spoke of animals, and when the author of Kings describes him doing this he suggests that Solomon is a new Adam (4:24, 33). In the Song of Songs, the builder of gardens and temples (cf. Eccles. 2:4-5), King Solomon, writes of the glory of relations between man and woman in a way that seeks to regain what was lost when humans were driven from Eden.

To read of the intimacy described in the Song of Songs is like entering the holy place where God walks in the cool of the day. Moses, who wrote the narratives concerning both Eden and the tabernacle, shaped those narratives to show that the tabernacle is a kind of new Eden.[9] With the imagery of the Song so reminiscent of Eden, the connection with the presence of God in Eden and the holy places in tabernacle and temple takes on tremendous significance. Prior to sin, the man and his wife dwelt in the presence of God, and they were naked and not ashamed (Gen. 2:25). We should think of human nakedness with neither the crude lust nor the fearful shame that lamentably characterize our fallen impulses. We should think of the naked intimacy of man and wife with the sober dignity that would befit those who stood before God unfallen in the edenic holy of holies.

Our culture suffers from a plague of pornography. Perhaps nothing more threatens the purity of the church today than the smut the world slobbers over. Freedom from the filth comes in the desire for a more powerful pleasure. The degrading, dehumanizing, objectifying prostitution of pleasure on offer from the world is a twisted perversion of the true satisfaction to be found in the enjoyment of God's good gift within the boundaries of God's good commandments.

Can you imagine what would it be like to stand naked, flawless, perfect, worshiping, without sin in the presence of God? What with everything 'very good' and with sin not having 'entered the world' and with man and woman 'not ashamed,' there would have been no leering, no sneaking another look, no nervous giggles, no inhibition, no self-conscious fear that one's appearance was less than desirable, no impulse toward inappropriate behavior, no lurking bad memories of past transgression. Everything would have been innocent: undefiled and appropriate, respectful and trusting, safe and pure, and the man and woman would have been aware that God made the world, planted the garden, shaped them for each other, and was coming to walk with them 'in the cool of the day' (Gen. 3:8).

But Eve was tempted and Adam sinned (Rom. 5:12; 1 Tim. 2:14). Immediately they took steps to hide themselves, to cover their nakedness (Gen. 3:6-7). In the words, 'and

---

9. That John understood this reality can be seen from the way he depicts the new Jerusalem of the new heaven and earth as a new holy of holies, the city being a perfect cube (Rev. 21:16). See James M. Hamilton Jr., *Revelation: The Spirit Speaks to the Churches*, Preaching the Word (Wheaton: Crossway, 2012), 381-9.

they knew that they were naked' in Genesis 3:7, we see that suddenly they became aware of themselves in a way they never had been before. After sinning, they knew that they were vulnerable. Having broken their troth with God, they immediately understood they could no longer maintain their troth with one another, that they must protect their most vulnerable and sacred parts from one another. They sensed a danger, whether from eyes or otherwise, they had not known prior to sin. In contrast with their former 'no shame' nakedness (2:25), after sin they knew shame, so 'they sewed fig leaves together and made themselves loincloths' (3:7).

That's the world we know. The world in which we live is the one with sin in it, the one over which God has spoken judgment. We have been driven from the Garden of Eden, and we are no longer naked in perfect innocence. We wear clothing that protects us from other people and from a world that has been subjected to futility, a world of scorching heat and biting cold, desert famine and whelming flood.

There is enmity between the seed of the woman and the seed of the serpent (Gen. 3:15), and thus sometimes our clothing is for battle. There is animosity between man and woman (Gen. 3:16), and our clothing always protects from prying eyes. And there is a curse on the land that fills it with thorn and thistle (Gen. 3:17-19), so our clothing protects us from the harsh world outside Eden.

In the Song of Songs, Solomon sings a melody rich with reminiscent beauty, a beauty that resonates with us, a haunting beauty so sharp it sometimes cuts us open and lays us bare with a longing for what we do not now have. The beauty of the Song of Songs has an Eden-like loveliness. It has a harmony, a radiance, a shining innocence with a man and woman gazing on one another's glory, without an indication of any shame.

The Song is showing us something that the words of the poem do not overtly say. That is, the Song presents us with a married couple gazing on one another as Adam and Eve must have in Eden. There is safety, security, fidelity, and enjoyment, and there is no taking more than the other would give, no wanting more than is needed, and no coercion or manipulation. In the poetry of this book we see a man and woman trusting one another, and we see that trust as the man and woman each describe the other with no indication of embarrassment or discomfort—and the descriptions can be read aloud in church without embarrassment and discomfort, too. This book shows us the glory of a good marriage.

There is an awesome glory here that transcends everything we have known or desired. In the poetry of the Song of Songs we have an impressionistic narrative that depicts a descendant of David who has overcome the alienation between himself and his wife, removed the hostility and mistrust by his loving words, worked and kept a cursed land such that it has become like the Garden of Eden. In the words of this book the man and the woman stand before one another naked and unashamed; theirs is a stunning renewal of Eden's lost glory.

The Song's Hero: David's Son, the new Adam

When God cursed the serpent He said that a seed of the woman would crush the serpent's head (Gen. 3:15).[10] That Moses means to present Eve looking for the seed of the woman promised in Genesis 3:15 can be seen from his account of her responses when her sons were born (Gen. 4:1, 25). Moses then traces the line of descent from Adam to Abram in the ten-member genealogies of Genesis 5 and 11, and Lamech's words in Genesis 5:29 present him looking for a rollback of the curse in Genesis 3:17-19.[11] The blessing of Abraham in Genesis 12:1-3 then answers the curses of Genesis 3:14-19 point for point.[12] The line of descent continues right down to King David, to whom remarkable promises are made in 2 Samuel 7. The covenant with David in 2 Samuel 7 invokes the blessing of Abraham from Genesis 12 at many points, showing that the author of Samuel intends the covenant with David to be understood as the means by which the blessing of Abraham would be accomplished. The biblical authors expected the blessing of Abraham, the promises of land, seed, and blessing, to be realized through the promised descendant of David.

---

10. James M. Hamilton Jr., 'The Skull Crushing Seed of the Woman: Inner-Biblical Interpretation of Genesis 3:15,' *The Southern Baptist Journal of Theology* 10, no. 2 (2006): 30-54.

11. See further Hamilton, *God's Glory in Salvation through Judgment*, 75-83.

12. For an exposition of this sentence, see James M. Hamilton Jr., 'The Seed of the Woman and the Blessing of Abraham,' *Tyndale Bulletin* 58 (2007): 253-73.

Solomon is in that line of promise. The Old Testament texts trace his genealogy all the way back to Adam. Obviously he does not turn out to be the one who *ultimately* fulfills the promise, but he was in the line of expectation and became a type of the one to come (cf. Matt. 12:42). Given the Scripture that would have been available to Solomon, a case can be made that Solomon understood that he was—at least in part—causing the promises to come to pass, by building the temple, for instance. David was told his seed would build the temple (2 Sam. 7:13). Given the typological similarities between Solomon and other figures in the line of promise, Solomon probably understood that the patterns of his life were pointing forward to one in whom they would be ultimately realized. The key point here has to do with the way that the curses of Genesis 3 will be overcome by the blessing of Abraham in Genesis 12, which will be brought into reality by the promised King from the line of David in 2 Samuel 7.

The Bible begins with the loss of Eden because of sin, the consequence of which will be death. The restoration to life and God's presence is the salvation promised. This salvation implies a rollback of the curses: the renewal of creation, the healing of relational dysfunction, and the removal of the curse from the land. All this, the Old Testament promises, will be accomplished by great David's greater Son.

This broader narrative, this world-defining story, with this hope for its grand resolution, lies behind the lyrics of the Bible's poets. The biblical authors wrote their work to be understood within the context of a meta-narrative that begins with the problem of human sin, sin that results in death: alienation from God, from other people, and from the world. The back-story informing the biblical authors also provides the big answer to the world's big problem, and that answer comes in the promise of the seed of the woman, seed of Abraham, seed of Judah, seed of David, who will crush the serpent's head, reopen the way to Eden, renew harmony and justice between people, and usher His own people into the very presence of God. In a word, the promise of the seed of the woman in Genesis 3:15 is the promise of *life* (cf. Gen. 3:20).

In the Song of Songs we have Solomon, the son of David, King in Jerusalem, describing an Eden-like intimacy between himself and his wife in an Eden-like setting.[13] Solomon knows what he is doing, and he intends to depict a glorious renewal, the consummation of the hopes of the people of God. Relational dysfunction removed, the desert blooms like the Garden of Eden in the presence of God under the hand of the new Adam through whom God has brought His promises to pass.

The Song's Meaning: Poetry, Allegory, Typology, Oh My!

Before we consider how the Song is intended to instruct us, we should summarize the lines of argument being presented:

1) The setting of the Song of Songs indicates that Solomon means to depict himself as a descendant of David who is working and keeping a garden-city, such that what was lost when Adam was driven from Eden is being recaptured by what the son of David is doing in Jerusalem, on Mount Zion which the Lord loves.

2) The plot of the Song of Songs indicates that Solomon means to depict himself and his wife renewing the unashamed intimacy that Adam and Eve lost when they sinned. This renewed intimacy is pure and undefiled, sinful tendencies and hostilities overcome by the son of David.

3) The hero of the Song of Songs is Solomon the son of David, who works and keeps the garden-city and overcomes the alienation between himself and his beloved, achieving a renewal of an Eden-like scene and Eden-like relations.

What did the Song's author intend to teach his audience, which includes us, through the poetic depiction of this protagonist at work in this plot taking place in this setting?

This discussion will focus on the way the Song functions at three levels: 1) the Song of Songs depicts human love between a man and a woman; 2) the man in the song typifies the coming Messiah; and 3) the canonical context of the Song points to a deeper, symbolic understanding of marriage as a kind of allegory for the love between God and His people.[14]

---

13. This is the point I seek to establish in Hamilton, 'The Messianic Music of the Song of Songs.'

14. I say this in spite of the fact that, as Dillard and Longman note, 'the allegorical approach is in disfavor with a large majority of the academic community' (Tremper Longman III and Raymond B. Dillard, *An Introduction to the Old Testament* [Grand Rapids: Zondervan, 2006], 295).

On what basis do I justify the claim that there are multiple layers of *author-intended* meaning in this Song? At least three reasons establish the warrant for these conclusions: First, we are dealing with poetry, and poetry is by nature deliberately evocative and suggestive. Second, biblical authors who wrote before and after Solomon produced material intended to function in ways that correspond to what I am arguing Solomon intended in the Song.[15] Third, from what Paul says about marriage in Ephesians 5 we can be confident that we are on safe ground when comparing human marriage to the covenant between God and His people.[16] What does the Song teach about the love between man and woman, the man who typifies the Messiah, and the allegorical understanding of marriage?

The Song is about the love between a man and a woman. It is about human marital love and its physical delights. This love is relished in the context of marriage, the Bible's only authorized context for expressions of physical intimacy between man and wife. That God would give such a gift and then encourage its enjoyment shows Him to be a God who seeks the satisfaction and delight of His creatures. God does not keep pleasure from His people, but creates gratuitous goodness and gives sound instruction on how to savor it.

We should also note, however, that the man in the Song isn't just anyone. The man in the Song is the son of David, the first king after David, the first son of David to reign after the promises about the seed of David in 2 Samuel 7. The hero of the Song is the son of David who typifies, anticipates *the* Son of David who will bring about the fulfillment of all the promises of God. What is typology? Typology involves historical correspondence and an increase in significance.

---

15. Against Estes: 'this song cycle was probably not intended to be construed as an allegory of divine love, although it has most often been read in that manner throughout its interpretative history,' in Fredericks and Estes, *Ecclesiastes and the Song of Songs*, 300. There is warrant in the text, particularly when read in canonical context, for the way the Song has predominantly been understood in Jewish and Christian interpretation. There have obviously been excesses, but this should not keep us from dealing with the fact that throughout the Scriptures marriage is used as a symbol of the relationship between God and His people.

16. I am thus very much in sympathy with the 'Christological and analogical' hermeneutic espoused for the interpretation of the Song by Mitchell, *Song of Songs*, 4, 14-66, passim.

There are ways that Solomon corresponds to David and to Adam, and as the patterns of events recur in history, they increase in importance. These historical correspondences and escalations in importance build up to Jesus, who matches and exceeds those who were before Him. Jesus fulfills the pattern, the type, that Solomon depicts in the Song of Songs. Jesus is the ultimate bridegroom (cf. Matt. 9:15; 25:1-13; John 3:29; 2 Cor. 11:2; Rev. 19:6-9; 21:2, 9; 22:17).[17]

I don't know about you, but when I look at the Song of Songs I wish I could have ideas this good. I wish I could always see the world beautiful, as the Song depicts it. I wish I could describe the world and my beloved in such expressive, creative, fresh ways. The poetry causes us to long to experience the beauty detailed by the book. It's better than we could have imagined, better than the way life typically goes for us. By showing us this better life, the Song shows us that we need the son of David, Solomon, who was inspired by the Holy Spirit, to show us this world. Even more, we need the Son of David, Jesus, who brought God's purposes to pass to make the glory of the Song a reality for us.

Jesus is the one who overcame the curses. Jesus is the one who accomplished redemption. Jesus is the one whose resurrection set the new creation in motion. Jesus is the one who opened the way to the new and better Eden. Jesus is the one we must trust if we want to enter that new Eden in the future and experience anticipations of it in the present. Jesus is the bridegroom (John 3:29). Jesus laid down His life for His bride, the church (Eph. 5:25). Jesus will consummate the new marriage, the new covenant, and we will celebrate the marriage feast of the lamb when He returns (Rev. 19:9).

If we want our marriages to approach what is depicted in the Song of Songs, we need to trust Jesus, to be enabled by His Spirit, and to follow in His footsteps by laying down our lives for our beloved.

---

17. I disagree with G. Lloyd Carr, who writes, 'the text of the Song gives no indication that it is intended as typology. The Song is presented simply as an account of the relationship between the lover and the beloved. Nor is there any indication in the New Testament that the Song has a Christological interpretation or application' (*The Song of Solomon*, Tyndale Old Testament Commentaries [Downers Grove: InterVarsity, 1984], 31). For a list of 'possible NT allusions and verbal parallels to the Song,' see Mitchell, *Song of Songs*, 29-34.

We have looked at the way the Song celebrates human love and the way Solomon typifies Jesus, but what about the allegorical meaning of marriage?[18] Dictionary.com defines 'allegory' as 'a representation of an abstract or spiritual meaning through concrete or material forms.'[19] Some allegorical interpretations of the Song of Songs have gone too far.[20] But modern interpreters have overreacted to allegorical excess by rejecting this aspect of the Song's meaning altogether. Paul, after all, does employ allegorical interpretation (Gal. 4:21-31).

We do not have to deny that the Song pertains to human love if we suggest that there is also a sense in which Solomon typifies Christ, nor do these two, the human-love interpretation *and* the Solomon-typifies-Christ reading, exclude the view that marriage is a picture of the covenant between God and His people. As early as Exodus 34:15, Israel is warned that those who worship the idols of the nations 'whore after their gods.' The view that the covenant between Yahweh and Israel is a marriage informs the widespread indictment of spiritual adultery in the Old Testament.

In the book of Hosea, Hosea represents the LORD in his marriage to Gomer, and Gomer represents Israel. Jeremiah and Ezekiel both develop this spiritual adultery extensively, and Jeremiah presents the LORD referring to Israel as 'my beloved', using the same root that occurs at many points in the Song of Songs (see the use of ידיד *yadid* in Jer. 11:15; 12:7, and the use of דּיד *dod* in Song 1:2, 4, 13, 14, 16 etc.). With the covenant between Yahweh and Israel being viewed as a marriage, and with the new covenant being treated as a new marriage (see esp. Hosea 2:14-23), we have reason to think that Old Testament authors, including Solomon, knew that human marriage pointed beyond itself to the relationship between God and His people.

---

18. Cf. Mitchell, *Song of Songs*, 89, where he writes, 'This commentary rejects pure allegory,' then describes an interpretation similar to what is proposed here, 89-93.

19. Cf. the definition provided by Clement Wood, *Poets' Handbook* (Cleveland: World, 1940), 415: 'An allegory is a presentation of a meaning implied, but not expressly stated. It is in essence a prolonged metaphor, in which actions symbolize other actions, and often the characters are types or personifications.'

20. Many will think of Origen here, on whom see the balanced biographical introduction in Joseph W. Trigg, *Origen*, The Early Church Fathers (New York: Routledge, 1998), 3-66, and for Origen's interpretation of the Song see pp. 45-9.

This possibility of a deeper meaning of marriage is augmented by the fact that there is another wedding song in the Bible, Psalm 45, where the king of Israel is identified with God. Psalm 45:1-5 extols the greatness of the Davidic King, and then verse 6 shows an extremely close connection between the throne of God and the throne of the Davidic King: 'Your throne, O God, is forever and ever. The scepter of your kingdom is a scepter of uprightness' (Ps. 45:6, esv).

This Psalm (that closely identifies Yahweh and the king from the line of David who represents Him) is referred to as 'a love song' in its superscription, and the lyrics go on to address a princess who appears to be the king's new bride from a foreign land (Ps. 45:10-17). Solomon himself famously married foreign princesses (1 Kings 3:1), a point of connection between the love song Psalm 45 and the love song that is the subject of this study.

The idea that the covenant between God and His people was understood as a marriage is firmly established. We add to this that the agent of that covenant who is closely identified with God is the anointed king from David's line, the Messiah. This would appear to provide a strong basis for Paul's words in Ephesians 5:32. Having quoted Genesis 2:24 in Ephesians 5:31, Paul writes in 5:32: 'This mystery is profound, and I am saying that it refers to Christ and the church' (esv). Paul seems to be asserting that marriage exists to portray the relationship between Christ and the church.[21] The poetry of the Song of Songs likewise has a meaning that plumbs deeper than merely human love, and I contend that Solomon *intended* his audience to see not only human love in the Song but also a typified Messiah and an allegorical correspondence with the relationship between God and His people.

The biblical authors indisputably knew an allegorical meaning of marriage. The application of the concrete reality of marriage to the spiritual relationship—the covenant—between God and His people can be found throughout the Bible. In the Old Testament, this spiritual reality takes the

---

21. For my attempt at a biblical-theological exposition of Ephesians 5, see James M. Hamilton Jr., 'The Mystery of Marriage,' in *For the Fame of God's Name: Essays in Honor of John Piper*, ed. Sam Storms and Justin Taylor (Wheaton: Crossway, 2010), 253-71.

form of the love between Yahweh and Israel and the marriage covenant they entered into at Sinai. In the New Testament, the same spiritual reality is fulfilled in the love between Christ and the church, His bride. The Song of Songs was intended by Solomon to stir up the longings of God's people for *the Messiah*, the Christ, the Bridegroom, God's image and likeness who comes as our covenant Lord to slay the dragon and win His bride, whom he marries by initiating the new covenant.

Conclusion

The Song of Solomon has a hero, the male figure in the Song, Solomon the son of David, who typifies the one to come. In the Song this type of Christ is overcoming the alienation and hostility between himself and his beloved. He is restoring the intimacy lost between man and woman when Adam and Eve sinned. He has cultivated a garden and built a city. He is providing an example for all husbands to follow, and the wife in the Song is likewise exemplary. We should follow the example of Solomon and the Shulammite as they point to the love between Christ and the church, and we should allow the love between Solomon and his bride depicted in this most sublime Song to point us beyond human marriage to its ultimate referent, the marital-covenant-love between Christ and the church.

There are practical realities that lend us specific applications here: God has inspired the Song of Songs to show us true love and to help us rightly order our relationships. Many people are drawn to perversions of God-honoring sexual expression because of the powerful pleasure and delight to be had, even from distortions of this gift of God. In the Song of Songs, God has shown us a blissful expression of marital love. God woos us away from sinful attempts at pleasure with a Song that sings the holy enjoyment of what He makes possible.

Have you ever wondered whether there could be anything better than perversion and smut? Has the disgusting, dehumanizing, degrading nature of the world's harlotry repulsed you? There is something better, and God reveals it to us through the inspiration of King Solomon, accomplishing it through King Jesus.

God calls us away from the powerful pleasure of sin with the depiction of the superior pleasures of holiness in this most sublime Song. God doesn't use a chisel to chip away at sexual perversion, He uses poetry set to music: The Song of Solomon.

QUESTIONS FOR DISCUSSION

1. How does the setting of the Song of Songs in Zion and a lush garden affect the way we think about what the poetry depicts between the King and his Bride?

2. Are there other texts in the Bible that are as reminiscent of the Garden of Eden as the Song of Songs seems to be?

3. The impressionistic plot of the Song of Songs moves from alienation and hostility to reconciliation and harmony. Is this pattern reflected elsewhere in the Bible? What do you think of the suggestion that this is the big story of the whole Bible?

4. The King in the Song is the son of David, Solomon. As we seek to imitate Christ, what can we learn from the negative and positive example set by Solomon?

5. This book takes the view that the most significant background for understanding the Bible's poetry is earlier Scripture. Does that differ from the way that you have thought about the Bible's poetry, or from the way you have heard others explain it?

2

The Exemplary King
(Song of Songs 1)

Main Point

In Song of Songs 1, we see the King[1] exemplifying the kind of godly character that produces from his Bride the response of loving longing and admiration.

Context

The Song of Songs is about human love, but the hero of the Song is no common man. He's the King of Israel, the son of David, and he is a Shepherd-King who has cultivated a garden-city, even as he overcomes the alienation and hostility between himself and his Bride to renew an Eden-like intimacy between them. The Song is about human love, and the son of David who is the King in the Song is a type of the one who is to come.

Marriage, moreover, has a deeper, symbolic meaning in the Old Testament, as the covenant between Yahweh and Israel is spoken of in marital terms. When that covenant was broken, God promised a new covenant in new marital terms (Hosea 2:18-20), and that new covenant is the one between Christ, the bridegroom, and the church, His bride. The Song

---

1. I will refer to the male figure in the Song as the King and to the female as the Bride. The conclusion that these two become man and wife as the poem unfolds will be reflected in the typographical convention of capitalizing the references to Bride and King, which in turn reinforces their identity as individuals. When quoting English translations, the lower case will be retained unless otherwise noted.

of Songs is thus about human love, about messianic hope, and about the covenant between God and His people, pointing to the new covenant, which Paul tells us is the real meaning of marriage (Eph. 5:32).

Preview

1:1   Title and Tie to the Canon

    1:2-7   The Bride and the Daughters of Jerusalem

    1:2-4a   The Bride Longing for the King

    1:4b   Daughters of Jerusalem

    1:5-7   The Bride to the Daughters and the Shepherd King

1:8-17 The King and the Bride

    1:8-11   The King to the Bride

    1:12-14   The Bride about the King

    1:15   The King to the Bride

    1:16   The Bride to the King

    1:17   The King about the Relationship

Song 1:1: Title and Tie to the Canon
'The Song of Songs, which is Solomon's.' Thus opens the most sublime Song. We read of Solomon in 1 Kings 4 that he 'spoke 3,000 proverbs, and his songs were 1,005' (1 Kings 4:32 [Masoretic Text (MT) 5:12]). We should also note that in 1 Kings 4 Solomon had dominion like Adam (1 Kings 4:24 [MT 5:3]; Gen. 1:26-28), Solomon named creation like Adam (1 Kings 4:33 [MT 5:13]; Gen. 2:19-20), and every man sat under his vine and fig tree (1 Kings 4:25 [MT 5:5]).

What would have been the subject of the 1,005 songs Solomon wrote? From the book of Proverbs we see that he was concerned with the raising of sons and daughters, wise dealing for people young and old, single or married, rich or poor. From Ecclesiastes we know that he considered frustration and satisfaction, vanity and significance, youth and old age, solitude and companionship. He thought, and thought well, about everything. He had the wisdom to ask God for 'a hearing heart' (1 Kings 3:9, my trans.), and the Lord gave him 'a heart of wisdom and understanding' (3:12), with the result that his 'breadth of heart was like the sand of the seashore' (4:29 [MT 5:9], my trans.) so that he could be described as 'wiser than all men' (4:31 [MT 5:11]).

When we consider something written by Solomon, we must recognize that we are looking at the work of a man of immense natural talent, the most brilliant mind of his day. Indeed, it would appear that this side of the incarnate Christ, Solomon's intellectual gifts surpassed all others, for the Lord said to him, 'Behold, I give to you a heart of wisdom and understanding, so that none like you has been before, and none like you shall arise afterward' (1 Kings 3:12).[2]

Even a man of great wisdom would have to apply himself to write 1,005 songs. With the responsibilities of leading the nation as king, with the building projects, and with all the domestic activity, it is not likely that Solomon wrote a song a day, but even producing them at that rate would require nearly three years of constant work to write a thousand songs. From this we can conclude that Solomon was years in the writing of these songs. He kept at it, probably over the course of his life: revising, crafting, planning, executing, revisiting, collecting words, themes, and ideas, watching for opportunities and waiting for the inspiration to come. After a few dozen songs, most of us would probably have exhausted our creativity, to say nothing of a few hundred. To keep producing songs would require attention to form and diligent work to hone craft. The artist who would create so much must discipline God-given talents.

Solomon's songs, proverbs, and reflections, then, are the work of a genius the like of which the world has not seen elsewhere. Solomon's writings are mature work, too, cultivated through disciplined practice and the steady application of enormous ability to produce works of truth, goodness, and beauty.

---

2. Cf. Garrett's remark that 'The high literary style of the Song suggests that it was written at a time when Israel had the means to and the motivation for literary pursuits' in Garrett and House, *Song of Songs, Lamentations*, 19.

To the unsurpassed God-given wisdom, the long practice, and the diligent labor necessary to produce over a thousand songs, we add the recognition that Solomon was inspired by the Holy Spirit in the writing of Proverbs, Song of Songs, and Ecclesiastes. These books deserve careful attention!

The title, 'Song of Songs,' tells us that of all the songs Solomon wrote, this was his pinnacle achievement. Solomon, the temple builder and student of holy Scripture, would be aware of the statement he was making as he affixed a title grammatically parallel to the 'holy of holies.' This song is the inner sanctum of his output, the most sublime of his songs.

Having rehearsed what happened to Israel in the wilderness, Paul told the Corinthians, 'Now these things happened to them typologically, but they were written for our instruction, upon whom the ends of the ages have come' (1 Cor. 10:11, my trans.). Solomon's own failures, detailed in 1 Kings 11, provide a cautionary tale, an example that we should not imitate. Books like Song of Songs and Ecclesiastes can be read as statements of repentance, indications that their author recognized how things should have gone and how he had failed. We should learn from the negative example, and we should learn from the positive.

Solomon's literary output is exemplary. He clearly worked long and hard to produce art for God's glory. We continue to benefit from his efforts today. Solomon considered how to stir others up to love and good deeds (cf. Heb. 10:24), and he gave the world three books of the Bible, three books that have been studied for the last three thousand years and that will be studied as long as people can breathe or eyes can see.

Are you an artist, a poet, a song-writer? Are you honing your craft? If a man of Solomon's gifts could apply himself with the diligence necessary to produce 3,000 proverbs and 1,005 songs, should not we of lesser natural gifting follow his example in the application of our abilities through diligence, study, and work to stir others up to love and good deeds for the glory of God? Given, too, that a Spirit-inspired genius worked hard to give us this best of his songs, should we not diligently apply ourselves to this Song? Should we not read and reread it, meditating on it, praying through it, thinking hard about its meaning?

The book's opening words tell us that this is the Song of Songs, and it is Solomon's. The name 'Solomon' in the first verse of this Song ties the book to the canon. This canonical link will also inform much of the imagery Solomon uses in the Song.

Why is it important to read the Song of Songs in light of the rest of the canon? Because, as I argued in the previous chapter, the Song is a poetic summary of the big story of the whole Bible, interpreting and contributing to the definitive explanation of the world.

The big story begins in a garden, with a man and woman naked without shame (Gen. 1–2; 2:25). The plot conflict comes when a beast, over whom the man has been given dominion (Gen. 1:26-28; 2:19-20), incites God's image and likeness to rebel against God, transgress God's command, and thereby put the snake in God's place (3:1-6). As God judges the serpent, God promises that a seed of the woman will crush the head of the serpent (3:15). Because of the sin of man, death is introduced to the world (cf. 2:17; 5:4, etc.), along with shocking changes in both the setting of the story and the relations between its characters and their costumes.

Because of their sin, the man and woman sought to clothe themselves (Gen. 3:7), hiding their nakedness from one another. Because of their sin, their relationship was made difficult, particularly as it related to childbearing for the woman, which is necessary for the carrying out of God's command for them to be fruitful and multiply (Gen. 3:16; cf. 1:28).[3] In addition, because of their sin, the ground was cursed, making the man's responsibility to work and keep it painful and difficult (Gen. 3:17-19; cf. 2:15). The word of judgment to the serpent means that in spite of their sin, the man and woman will continue to live, they will have children, and their seed will defeat the serpent.[4] In response to this, Adam names the woman 'mother of all living' (3:20), and at the birth of Noah, Lamech indicates that he is hoping for a day when the curses of Genesis 3:14-19 will be rolled back (5:29, cf. 3:17-19). They

---

3. For exploration of these ideas, see my essay, 'A Biblical Theology of Motherhood.'

4. The reverberation of Genesis 3:15 through the canon is the subject of my essay, 'The Skull Crushing Seed of the Woman.'

are nevertheless banished from the garden, and God Himself clothed them with garments of skin (3:21-24).

The line of descent from Adam and Eve is carefully traced because of the all-important promise about the seed of the woman. A ten-member genealogy from Adam to Noah comprises Genesis 5, and another ten-member genealogy goes from Noah's son Shem to Abram in Genesis 11. The blessings of Abraham in Genesis 12:1-3 then answer the curses of Genesis 3:14-19 point for point.[5] The hope of the world, and the resolution of the plot of the Bible's big story, hinges on the seed of the woman who will bring to pass the blessing of Abraham, a blessing that promises his seed will restore God's blessing to the land.

These themes from Genesis are relevant to our study of the Song of Songs because the covenant with David in 2 Samuel 7 is layered onto the blessings of Abraham from Genesis 12:1-3, making it clear that the seed of David whom the Lord will put on His throne is also the seed of Abraham who will bring blessing to the land, who is also the seed of the woman who will crush the head of the serpent. Solomon is not the ultimate realization of these hopes, but he typifies the one whom the Lord will raise up to bring the promises to fulfillment.

The Song of Songs is a poetic depiction of the seed of David overcoming alienation between himself and his beloved to restore intimacy, indeed nakedness without shame, and the setting of this Song alternates between a lush garden reminiscent of Eden and David's capital city, Jerusalem, Mount Zion which the Lord loves.[6] This is the big-story backdrop against which we must read this book. To change the metaphor, the Bible's big themes build the concert hall that provides the author-intended acoustic context in which the Song of Songs is to be heard. This is the big story to which Solomon's name links us, the big story the imagery of the Song summarizes and interprets, the big story whose plot resolution is the culmination of the longings aroused by this most sublime Song.

---

5. I discuss this further in, 'The Seed of the Woman and the Blessing of Abraham.'

6. For an article-length look at the Song from this perspective, see my study, 'The Messianic Music of the Song of Songs.'

Having considered how the first verse ties this book to the rest of the biblical canon, let's look at the interaction between the Bride and the Daughters of Jerusalem in Song 1:2-7.

Song 1:2-7: The Bride and the Daughters of Jerusalem
Song 1:2-4a, The Bride Longing for the King
As we consider Song 1:2, let me invite you to consider what kind of man causes a woman to feel what the Bride articulates here. I don't think this is raw physical attraction, because elsewhere in the Song appearances are described whereas here the statement that explains why she wants him to kiss her is that his *love* is better than wine. So the focus here seems to be on the Bride responding to how the King loves her.

The King treats her in such a way that she wants him to kiss her. Note that what the Bride says in 1:2-4 seems to indicate that she is musing on the King, perhaps in the company of the daughters of Jerusalem (1:5). Again we're dealing with poetry, which is more impressionistic than a narrative telling us who is where, but I say this because she begins to speak of him in the third person: 'Let *him* kiss me ...' in the first line of verse 2; then she switches to the second person in the second line of verse 2, 'For *your* love ...' So perhaps she sits musing with her friends and he is elsewhere or across the room. She begins by reflecting on him and continues by addressing him.

She explains her desire to be kissed in the first line of Song 1:2 with three statements, the first of which is in the second line of verse 2, 'For your love is better than wine.' Proverbs 5:19-20 also speaks in terms of marital love being intoxicating. There is a happiness, a buzz, an excitement that results from marital love that is better than what people seek from wine.

Her second reason is in the first line of verse 3, 'your anointing oils are fragrant.' I think there is more than one connotation here. On the one hand, no doubt the King's scent is pleasing to her nostrils, but on the other hand, this is the King of Israel she is addressing, the Lord's *Anointed*. The same term used for 'oil' in the passages describing the anointing of David and Solomon (1 Sam. 16:1; 1 Kings 1:39, *shemen*) is used here. So what the Bride says here could point beyond mere pleasing aromas to a recognition of the significance of the anointed King of Israel, pointing to an appreciation of his role in God's purposes.

The third reason in the second line of 1:3 also speaks of oil, but it adds something that ties into the blessing of Abraham and the covenant with David. God told Abraham that He would make his *name* great (Gen. 12:2), and Nathan told David that Yahweh would make his name like Abraham, Isaac, and Jacob's: 'I will make for you a great name, like the name of the great ones of the earth' (2 Sam. 7:9). Psalm 72 is a prayer about the reign of David's son, Solomon (cf. its superscription and verse 20), and in Psalm 72:17 we read, 'May his name endure forever.' These considerations lead me to think that when Solomon depicts the Bride speaking of the King's 'oils' and then saying 'your name is oil poured out' in Song 1:3, there are strong connotations of the blessing of Abraham being fulfilled in the son of David. The Old Testament hope is for the blessing of Abraham to be realized through the King from David, and that hope seems to be poetically invoked here in the Song.

These connotations of the blessing of Abraham and the son of David inform the Bride's conclusion at the end of Song 1:3. Having detailed three reasons why she wants him to kiss her, she concludes at the end of verse 3, 'therefore virgins love you.' He is desirable, and he is significant in the purposes of God. In Luke 1 we see Mary amazed that God would show her the favor of giving her the privilege of being the mother of the long-awaited Messiah (Luke 1:46-49), and then Elizabeth blesses her, asking, 'why is this granted to me that the mother of my Lord should come to me' (1:41-43). There was likely a similar sentiment among the young women of Israel in Solomon's day: a longing that they might be like Sarah, Rebekah, and even Ruth, married to the man through whom God's promise would be realized, giving birth to the promised seed of the woman.

Obviously the King is depicted in the Song as a wonderful person with a stellar reputation. He is depicted as desirable. But the language used in Song 1:2-3 hints at more than the mere attractions of character and reputation, suggesting a recognition of the King's place in the promises and purposes of God.

The Bride then expresses her desire to be *alone* with the King in verse 4, 'Draw me after you; let us run. The king has brought me into his chambers' (Song 1:4). Should we take the second line of verse 4 to indicate that the Bride and the King are now in the King's chambers? Because of the near and broad context, the answer appears to be no. It seems that the daughters of Jerusalem speak in the rest of verse 4, then the Bride speaks to them in verse 5; thus it does not appear that the Bride has indeed been taken into the King's chambers where they are alone together. Then in the broader context, the consummation of the marriage seems to be celebrated in 4:16–5:1. For these reasons Bride and King are likely not alone in the King's chambers in Song 1:4. In the company of her friends, the Bride has spoken of her longing as though it has come to pass.

Before we move on to the rest of verse 4, let's take stock of what we've seen so far in Song 1:2-4a. The Bride longs for the King. Solomon depicts this Bride longing for face-to-face intimacy with the King because of his character, because of his place in God's purposes, and because of his reputation, and she acknowledges that she is the Bride whose Groom the virgins love. Application? At the level of human love, men, we can take stock of our character and ask ourselves whether our wives think of us this way. If they don't, what can we change about our character and conduct in order to be this kind of man? This is not a legalistic application. The King in the Song is a type of Christ. Those who are redeemed by the blood of Christ are called to follow in His footsteps (1 Pet. 2:21), loving their wives as Christ loved the church (Eph. 5:25).

As we have seen, these opening verses of the Song contain messianic connotations, connections to the blessing of Abraham and the covenant with David's anointed son. If marriage is, as Paul tells us, ultimately about Christ and the church (Eph. 5:32), the church would do well to imitate what we see the Bride doing here. Paul describes the Corinthians as waiting for the revealing of the Lord Jesus (1 Cor. 1:7; cf. 1 Thess. 1:10), speaks in 2 Timothy 4:8 of those who love the appearing of Jesus, and Hebrews 9:28 says Jesus is coming 'a second time ... to save those who are eagerly waiting for him.' Are you eagerly waiting for Jesus? Do you love and long for His appearing? If you're part of the Bride of Christ, if you belong to the church, you should. How can we grow in this longing? By the Word of God and prayer. Ask the Lord to give you a deeper love for Jesus, a better understanding of His significance and character and desirability. And read the Bible. Memorize the Bible. Meditate on the Bible. O, how we need the Bible.

We hear from the daughters of Jerusalem in the rest of Song 1:4.

Song 1:4b, Daughters of Jerusalem

The daughters of Jerusalem speak in 1:4b, and then the Bride addresses them in 1:5. The daughters of Jerusalem say, 'We will exult and rejoice in you; we will extol your love more than wine; rightly do they love you' (Song 1:4b—note the first-person plurals in this statement). The last statement, 'rightly do they love you,' may be the beginning of the Bride's words, which will continue in 1:5-7. Every 'you' in this statement in Song 1:4b is a masculine singular, which means that the daughters of Jerusalem are addressing the King. They rejoice in him, extol his love more than wine (cf. 1:2, 4), and love him rightly. Because this love for the King is upright ('rightly do they love you'), we are not dealing here with the daughters of Jerusalem jealously desiring the Bride's groom but with them appropriately admiring the King. This adds to the messianic overtones of the passage. Whereas it might not be appropriate for young single women to rejoice in another woman's husband, if that husband is the King of Israel, the anointed of the Lord, the son of David who will bring about the blessing of Abraham, we can understand why the young women could rightly love him though he is the husband of another.

Song 1:5-7, The Bride to the Daughters and the Shepherd King

At this point a note of tension is sounded in the Song. We have seen the title and the longing of the Bride, and now we hear something like fear. There is uncertainty and insecurity as the Bride raises questions about whether her appearance is what it needs to be. She starts in Song 1:5 by describing how she is dark, addressing the daughters of Jerusalem, then she implores them not to gaze at her because she is dark in verse 6 (this imperative is a plural, indicating that she addresses a group; it's a masculine, which may include the King with the daughters). She explains in verse 6 that she is dark because she has had to keep the vineyards, apparently meaning that she had to work in the sun and developed a tan, such that she could not keep her own vineyard, meaning that she could not preserve herself untanned.

Verse 7 continues this note of vulnerability: she is vulnerable because of her dark complexion, and she is vulnerable because she wants to find the King as he shepherds his flock at noon but does not want to appear 'like one who veils herself' (Song 1:7). This phrase is reminiscent of the way that Tamar veiled herself in Genesis 38:14, which suggests that in making this request the Bride seeks to protect her reputation in the community. The fact that the King is a shepherd adds a pastoral overtone to his role that is reminiscent of Moses and David. This is a shepherd King.

The description of the King shepherding his flock in Song 1:7 invites us to consider the way that Solomon depicts himself in the Song (cf. the use of his own name in Song 3:7, 9, 11, etc.). It seems unlikely that the historical Solomon was actively engaged in shepherding a flock. His father David was king in Jerusalem, and while David himself had served as a shepherd in his youth, by the time Solomon was born David was ensconced in the palace in Zion. These realities suggest that the depiction of Solomon as a shepherd is intended to link him to the shepherd leaders of Israel's history, men like Abel, Joseph, Moses, and David. This also indicates that in the Song Solomon is not presenting *historical narrative* but *idealized poetry*. As we continue through the Song I will point to other indications that Solomon is not writing a biographical account of what took place in his life in this Song. Instead, Solomon seems to present a stylized, typological portrait of himself, and the Solomon of the Song is a better man than the historical Solomon (cf. his fall into polygamy that led to idolatry in 1 Kings 11:1-8). We should not take this as an attempt to whitewash history but read it as Solomon's recognition of his own failure and his affirmation of the goodness of God's instructions. Solomon presents an idealized version of himself, typifying and pointing forward to the one in whom God's promises will be realized.

The Bride's vulnerability about her appearance and concern for her standing in the community will be resolved by the confidence-inspiring assurances the King gives her as he addresses her concerns in Song 1:8-11.

Song 1:8-17: The King and the Bride

In verses 8-17, the King will answer the Bride's concerns (Song 1:8-11), prompting the Bride to speak with confidence of the joy of their relationship (1:12-14). Then follows a back-and-forth with King and Bride exchanging compliments, culminating in each describing their relationship in terms of green and verdant fertility, as though to depict an 'arbor of trees as their home' (Brown-Driver-Briggs [BDB], s.v. ברות, *berot*, used in 1:17). It is almost as though the King's reassuring words join with the Bride's statement of their love to bring them home to Eden.

1:8-11, The King to the Bride

The King's opening words in verse 8 address both of the Bride's concerns. He says to her, 'If you do not know, O most beautiful among women, follow in the tracks of the flock, and pasture your young goats beside the shepherds' tents' (Song 1:8). By immediately giving her the information she needs to avoid being 'like one who veils herself,' the King addresses her concern about her standing and reputation. By addressing her as the 'most beautiful among women' he alleviates any concern she may have about her 'dark' appearance.

In order for the King to have addressed her concerns, he had to listen to her. He heard what her concerns were, and his love for her prompted him to address those concerns. The King's attentive responsiveness to his Bride in the Song should stir men who would love the way he does to listen, pay attention, and address the concerns of the beloved.

The King gives the Bride the assurance she needs, and he also gives her the information she needs to find him, implicitly inviting her to do so. Because of the possible associations and imagery suggested, it is noteworthy that in 1:5 the Bride refers to 'tents and curtains' and now in 1:8 we have a reference to 'tents.' Because of the way similar imagery will recur through the Song (cf. esp. 3:7-11), these terms might introduce subtle connotations of the dwelling place of God, the tabernacle and later the temple built by Solomon.

The King then extols the beauty of the Bride. He begins by likening the Bride to a lovely mare in Song 1:9. I sometimes wonder whether modern readers who express surprise over such a comparison have ever actually looked at a horse. They really are beautiful, graceful animals, and this comparison is both creative and flattering. Its freshness is part of its appeal. It draws our minds both to the graceful beauty of a woman and the loveliness of a mare, enabling us to see things new. The King goes on to speak of the way the Bride's beauty is augmented by jewels in Song 1:10, and then it could be the King speaking in the royal 'we' in verse 11, communicating what he intends to have done for the Bride, or perhaps another group joins in the celebration of the Bride.

The King's words have set the Bride at ease regarding the concerns she communicated in Song 1:5-7, as we see from what she says in 1:12-15. Before we move on to what she says, however, let's pause and consider how Song 1:5-11 might be applied to both human love and to the relationship between Christ and the church.

At the level of human love, let's observe that the Bride communicates vulnerably. She speaks in verses 5-7 of things that really concern her, things that relate to her appearance, her standing in the community, and her access to the King. The King's reply to the Bride addresses these concerns. He has *listened* to her, and he's figured out what the issues are. He tells her where she can find him. He's accessible to her. He removes her concern about how she will appear in the community, and he assures her that she has nothing to fear about her appearance.

Married people, how are you talking to each other? Are you communicating what really concerns you? Are you being vulnerable with your spouse? And I would ask the husbands in particular: are you listening? Are you hearing what your wife is really saying? Single people, too, can learn to communicate from this passage.

At the level of the relationships between Christ and the church, brothers and sisters, do you have concerns about how you will appear before the judgment seat? Do you feel guilt or insecurity? Let the Lord Jesus wash you in the water of His Word: Paul says that what Jesus did has removed spot, stain, wrinkle, and blemish from His Bride, and he says that Jesus laid down His life to present the church to Himself in glory (Eph. 5:26-27). If you believe in Jesus, you are clean. You are forgiven.

If you're not a believer, won't you believe in Jesus? Won't you hear the words of Christ and let Him address your insecurity and fear? Won't you come to the baptismal waters to be plunged into His death and brought up in His life? Jesus is King, and He tells us how to find Him. He tells us to remain in His Word (John 15:1-7). He will make us holy that we might enter the presence of His Father. We need only hear His Word and trust Him.

1:12-14, The Bride about the King

In verse 12, the Bride speaks of herself as a fragrant aroma filling a room with the King reclining on his couch. This seems to be a way for her to describe the way that she adorns the King and augments his presence. Then in verse 13 she speaks of the King as a fragrant aroma to her, like a small bag of perfume tied around her neck, resting on her chest, making her more pleasing to herself and others. Each is a blessing to the other, and each makes the other more fragrant to other people as well.

Then in verse 14 the Bride speaks of the King as being 'a cluster of henna blossoms in the vineyards of Engedi.' David lived in the strongholds of Engedi as he avoided capture by Saul (1 Sam. 23:29). In this comparison, the Bride likens her beloved to fruitful flowers from a fertile field associated with King David.

If you're a single person looking for a spouse, this is what you want. You want someone who will not be smoke in your nostrils, someone who will not be a stench to your whole family. You want someone who will be like a fragrant aroma to you and others. And this is what you want to be, as a single person, as you prepare for marriage. You want to be a blessing to everyone. You want everyone to think, figuratively speaking, that the world smells better when you are near.

Wives, do you speak of your husbands in this way? Husbands, do you speak of your wives in this way? Solomon depicts these people talking about each other like this to model for us a new way of thinking about and referring to our spouses. And from what we see in 1:15-16, Solomon presents the King as the one who sets the tone.

1:15, The King to the Bride
Note that what the King says to the Bride in the opening words of verse 15 is exactly repeated in what the Bride says to the King in the opening words of verse 16. This King is setting an example that his Bride is following. Husbands, what kind of example are you setting for your wives? Wives, are you following the good example your husbands are setting?

We should note, too, that when he tells her she is beautiful here in 1:15, he specifically likens her eyes to doves. The eyes are a window to the soul, and they reflect a person's character and personality. The King will delight in all the loveliness of his Bride, but here he begins with her eyes.

1:16, The Bride to the King
The Bride's response in 1:16 begins with speaking the King's own words from 1:15 back to him (the wording is exactly the same in Hebrew, with the only exception of a masculine rather than a feminine grammatical form). She makes a statement at the end of verse 16 that connotes at least two things. She says their 'couch is green' (Song 1:16, ESV). The 1984 NIV rendered this, 'our bed is verdant.' On the one hand this communicates fertility, life. Like a well-watered garden with flowers and fruit, their place of repose teems with life-giving love. And on the other hand, as I mentioned earlier, the garden imagery of her statement combines with what I take to be his statement in verse 17.

1:17, The King about the Relationship
In 1:17 the King speaks of the beams and rafters of their home in the language of strong and healthy trees. This is garden

language. It is as though this marriage is moving in the direction of the Garden of Eden.

Conclusion

In the poetry of the Song of Songs, the King of Israel conducts himself toward his beloved such that their relationship renews the lost lushness of Eden. Solomon's intent seems to have been the presentation of the King in the Song as an exemplary husband.[7] Solomon shows the King's words giving assurance to his Bride about her insecurity, removing her doubt and granting her confidence in herself, access to him, and standing before others. Solomon understood that husbands have the ability to grant all this to their wives, if they will love them, if they will listen to them, and if they will speak as they should.

Solomon also understood the big story that was unfolding across the pages of the Old Testament. This story began in a garden, but because of sin people were driven from God's presence, driven out with a promise about a descendant who would arise and defeat evil and restore God's reign over God's world. Solomon wrote this Song to summarize, interpret, and contribute to that hope. He depicted the son of David bringing to pass the promises to Abraham, with the result that the King and his Bride enjoy an edenic relationship.

This is exactly what Jesus does for His people. Jesus is the King who laid down His life for His Bride. Those who walk with Jesus now find their lives to be like Eden, and when He comes again He will make all things new. He will make the desert bloom, and the new creation will be a better Eden.

If you want that for your life, if you want to walk with Jesus and have Him as your Lord and King, let me direct you back to Song 1:8, where the King instructs the Bride to 'follow in the tracks of the flock, and pasture your young goats beside the shepherds' tents.' Find a flock at a local church where Jesus is the good shepherd. The word 'pastor' is an old word that means 'shepherd.' Are you part of a flock whose shepherds are leading Christ's sheep toward the land of promise, the

---

7. Cf. the argument for a similar dynamic in the Psalms made by Jamie A. Grant, *The King As Exemplar: The Function of Deuteronomy's Kingship Law in the Shaping of the Book of Psalms*, Academia Biblica (Atlanta: Society of Biblical Literature, 2004).

new heaven and earth, the new Eden? Find a church and join yourself to those who long for the coming of the King.

QUESTIONS FOR DISCUSSION

1. 1 Peter 2:21 says that we are to follow the example Jesus set. Paul called the Corinthians to follow his example of following Christ (1 Cor. 11:1). If Jesus can refer to Himself as 'greater than Solomon' (Matt. 12:42), does this mean that where Solomon sets a good example we should follow in his foot-steps?

2. Have you practiced something long enough to have produced a body of work like Solomon's 1,005 songs? Could you identify your best? What steps should you take to pursue the kind of discipline that would make such an output possible?

3. If you are married or dating, are you paying the kind of attention to your spouse or potential spouse that would make it possible for you to address that person's deepest concerns about your relationship?

4. Are you cultivating an ability to communicate your love for your spouse in new and fresh ways?

5. When you think of relational harmony with your spouse, or if you are single, when you consider the marital harmony you hope others will enjoy, what categories inform your expectations and aspirations for yourself and others? Do you think of the situation in the Garden of Eden before sin?

3

The Flower and the Fruit Tree
(Song of Songs 2)

Our culture is awash in images of women, images of men, and images of men and women together in unrealistic ways. Life isn't like the movies or the magazines. Marriage isn't like the movies and the magazines. Where are we to go for a vision of what life *is* like, of what marriage *should* be? How are we to reorient our desires and recalibrate our expectations so that we want what we should want rather than the distortion the world offers?

Need
Is there any hope? Can satisfaction be had? What is it you desire? How would you fill in the blank in this sentence: My marriage would be exactly what I have always wanted if I could have ... what?

Men, do you want your wives to be different somehow? Ladies, do you want your husbands to be different somehow? Single folks, do you have expectations about what marriage will be like?

I suspect the ladies don't have trouble imagining how the men would like for them to be different, and if that's the case, men, and it involves them being a way they don't want to be, you need to take responsibility for the situation, stop being selfish, and love your wife. Convince her that you love her.

And men, I wonder if you can imagine how your wives would like for you to be different? I wonder if you care how they would like for you to be? Do you think of her? Is she convinced that you think of her and care about what she wants?

Main Point

The second chapter of the Song of Songs shows a woman's response to a man who protects her, provides for her, and woos her.

Context

As we have noted, this book is a *Song* that is *in the Bible*. Though we have divided up this Song into chapters to get it into manageable portions, we should recognize that there is a unity here: chapter two carries forward the dialogue at the end of chapter one. There is, however, a shift at the chapter break.

The repartee at the end of chapter one involved the King and Bride praising one another in back-and-forth fashion in 1:12-17. That back-and-forth continues in 2:1-2, and then the Bride speaks throughout 2:3–3:11. In 2:10-14 (15?), the Bride relates the King's words to her, but the King does not speak again until 4:1.

In 2:1-3 the Bride and the King speak of one another in metaphorical terms that continue the imagery of 1:16-17. In 1:16-17 their couch and house are described as an arbor of trees in a lush garden, and now in 2:1-2 the Bride will be praised as a flower in that garden, while the King is a protective fruit tree in that garden. This resumes imagery introduced in 1:13 when she called him 'myrrh,' and then in 1:14 she called him 'a cluster of henna blossoms.'

These godly people who are loving one another and experiencing a renewal of lost edenic intimacy are like trees in a garden planted by the Lord. It is almost as though they envision themselves as having been planted in the Garden of Eden (cf. Ps. 1:3).

Preview

> Song 2:1-3, The Flower and the Fruit Tree
>
> Song 2:4-7, The Bride's Longing and Warning
>
> Song 2:8-17, The Song of Spring

Song 2:1-3: The Flower and the Fruit Tree

Their home has just been described as a cultivated bower of strong green trees in 1:16, and now the Bride describes herself in 2:1 as a rose and a lily. Since there are two different flowers here, this is obviously not to be understood literally. Figuratively, metaphorically, their home is a garden bower and she is a blossom within it. She seems to be recognizing her role and function and communicating with confidence, confidence based on the King's compliments (cf. 1:5-11).

In 2:2 the King responds to her self-description and redirects it to celebrate how she is uniquely desirable to him. He takes her description of herself as a lily and says that if she's a lily, all other young women are brambles. The point is that she is uniquely attractive to him.

I recently listened to a recorded audiobook of Charlotte Brontë's novel, *Jane Eyre*. The novel tells the story of the love between Jane Eyre and Edward Fairfax Rochester. Brontë presents neither Jane Eyre nor Mr Rochester as physically attractive. In fact, early in their relationship, to test her honesty, Mr Rochester asks Jane if she finds him handsome. She tells him that he is not physically handsome, and he appreciates her honesty and integrity because he knows he is not handsome. Both Jane Eyre and Mr Rochester have the opportunity to marry people who *are* handsome. Everyone expects Mr Rochester to marry a beautiful young lady of his own social station, but this young lady is proud and neither her character nor her personality suit Mr Rochester. Jane has the opportunity to marry a young clergyman with the looks of a Greek god, but his presence is oppressive to her.

What is fascinating in this novel is the way that Mr Rochester and Jane fall madly, passionately, genuinely in love for one another, and it is a love that transcends physical beauty. Brontë shows through the story that to choose physical beauty over the genuine companionship Jane and Mr Rochester share would be a cheap and tawdry move that would demean them both, giving happiness to neither.

Charlotte Brontë establishes that neither Mr Rochester nor Jane is beautiful by physical standards, and then she shows the beauty of character each possesses and the joy they find in one another. She then relates how each comes to see the other as beautiful.

My point in relating these details comes down to this assertion based on the novel *Jane Eyre*: the character of the beloved transforms the perception of beauty.

Married men, if you don't look at your wife and say to her what Song of Songs 2:2 says, you need to repent. You need to stop looking as man looks, on the outward appearance, and you need to start looking as the Lord looks. You need to cultivate physical attraction for your wife and for her alone. Pursue your wife. Pray for the Lord to work in you such that she is the only woman in the world that you find to be physically attractive—whatever she looks like! And then steadfastly refuse to tolerate any lustful attraction for other female beauty. You can appreciate beauty without lusting, but if you feed your lust you will make the monster strong and large to devour you. Fight it. Love your wife. Live like she's a lily among brambles. Talk to her that way. Talk about her that way. Honor her. Don't you dare tell other people you wish she looked or acted some other way. If you have such thoughts, they will show. Drive those thoughts out. Slay them. She's united to you body and soul. Love her like your own flesh, and love her alone.

As we saw in Song of Songs 1, where the King praised the Bride, and in response the Bride praised the King, so now that he has praised her in 2:2, she praises him in 2:3. Solomon presents the Bride saying of the King, 'As an apple tree among the trees of the forest, so is my beloved among the young men.' It is interesting to observe how the figurative language is in line with the roles given to men and women. She is a lily, an adorning blossom in their garden bower, and he is a fruit tree. He is strong with roots to protect against violent winds, with leafy branches for shade against the sun, and he's bearing fruit that is both nourishing and delightful. And just as he has indicated his unique delight in her, so she chooses to sit only in his shade.

In what she says in 2:3, 'With great delight I sat in his shadow, and his fruit was sweet to my taste,' she indicates her happiness in his protection and provision. Notice that she is not constrained to sit in his shade but does so on her own initiative, because she delights to do so.

I want to be very delicate in what I am about to say. Some will be aware of other connotations that have been suggested by the second half of Song 2:3. If you have no idea what I'm talking about, don't let that trouble you. Reflection on these statements in Song of Songs 2 and the suggestions some have made has led me to the following conclusions. First, I am not convinced by the arguments for the view that physical consummations of the relationship between the King and the Bride are depicted in every chapter of the Song. As we saw with 1:4, which some suggest indicates that the Bride has been taken by the King into his private chambers, the fact that the daughters of Jerusalem speak in the second half of 1:4 and that the Bride addresses them in 1:5 indicates rather that she is in public, with other people, speaking of her longing for a coming consummation. Similarly, in 2:4 the Bride will speak of the King taking her to the banqueting house, and she will again address the daughters of Jerusalem in 2:7, so here again it seems that these scenes are taking place with others around. While there is not a specific, historical narrative in the Song, there is a symbolic, poetic progression. Solomon creates the impression that the couple are moving toward marriage, with the wedding day in 3:11 and the consummation in 4:16–5:1. If this is correct, because this book is in the Bible, and it is in the Bible because it was inspired by the Holy Spirit, no suggestion that Solomon hints at physical acts of intimacy prior to marriage is plausible in the least.

Second, notice that the Bride is speaking in 2:3, and notice that she is speaking of her delight. She gives every indication that she feels safe, secure, and pleased. There is no indication that the fruit tree has cajoled the flower into sitting in his shade and enjoying his fruit. I read a transcript of the comments of one well-known pastor who suggested that this verse could be used to constrain wives to do something they might not otherwise be inclined to do. Using this verse for that purpose is *antithetical* to what this poetry depicts and teaches.

In this poetic depiction, the flower is describing the way the fruit tree made her feel safe, secure, and pleased, but not the way the fruit tree used a Bible verse like the lever Archimedes said he could use to move the earth, to get the flower to do what he wanted. To do that would be to misuse this verse, to misunderstand the kind of relationship the Bride and King have, and to think about marriage in a selfish, un-Christlike way.

Away with the prudish rejection of the delights of physical intimacy in marriage. But let us be just as strong in our repudiation of selfish attempts to manipulate the beloved, to use the Bible to compel an undesired course of action. We want husbands and wives to know the kind of intimacy that we see in the Song of Songs, an intimacy that is possible because the man has protected, provided for, and wooed his wife, with the result that she feels safe, satisfied, and happy. This is an intimacy like what Jesus makes possible between Himself and His people because He is so trustworthy and such a good provider. That's the kind of husband men should want to be. That's the kind of intimacy we want to know.

Song 2:4-7: The Bride's Longing and Warning

The Bride has begun to speak in 2:3, and she will continue to speak through to the end of chapter 3, though again, in 2:10-14 she recounts the King's words to her. The plant and garden, tree and flower metaphors that we have seen in 2:1-3 now recede and the Bride will speak of herself and the King in human terms in 2:4-7.

The Bride says in Song 2:4, 'He brought me to the banqueting house, and his banner over me was love.' This reference to a 'banqueting house,' literally, 'house of wine,' seems to be a place where the King is holding a feast, and since 2:4 goes on to relate, 'and his banner over me was love,' it would appear that this is a public feast. Banners are things people are meant to see. So it seems that what the Bride is saying in verse 4 is that there was a feast in the King's hall where the King publicly displayed his love for his Bride. This would seem to refer to the way the King treats the Bride in public.

He conducts himself in such a way that his actions can be described as a banner of love that he waves over her for all to see.

The Bride goes on to make a statement in Song 2:5 that is appropriate for polite company but that could be taken to be very suggestive. As often happens in the Song, the words used are entirely safe, altogether appropriate, the kind of thing one could say in front of one's mother with a straight face, and yet at the same time these words could communicate more. These words could be taken as an innuendo, an indirect intimation or insinuation. The Bride says in 2:5, 'Sustain me with raisins; refresh me with apples, for I am sick with love,'—at least, that's one way this line could be translated (so ESV). It could also be rendered, 'cause me to lie down on raisins, spread me out on apples.' I think this is equivalent to the way that someone might say in English, as an expression of surprise, 'Well, lay me down.' Depending on the context, it could be suggestive of more than merely that the speaker has seen something impressive.

In Hosea 3:1, Israel is indicted for going after cult prostitutes (cf. Hosea 4:13-14), and apparently they would eat 'cakes of raisins' in these fertility rites (Hosea 3:1). I would take that to be a perversion of the righteous celebration of the kind of love feast that we see the Bride describing here in Song 2:5 when she wants to be sustained with raisins. Raisins are probably viewed as an aphrodisiac, and here the Bride wants her righteous love and desire for her husband to be maintained and renewed, whereas Hosea 4 describes a twisted version of the corruption of marital intimacy.

Song of Songs 2:6-7 is repeated later in the book in 8:3-4. Given the public context here in Song of Songs 2, perhaps the King has wrapped his arms around the Bride in a way that is appropriate at a feast before other people. This feast at the banqueting hall in Song 2:4 may in fact be part of a week-long marriage feast. The celebration lasted a week when Jacob married Leah in Genesis 29:27-28, and there seems to be another seven-day wedding feast in Judges 14:12. In view of what seems to be the public setting of these words, when she says, 'His left hand is under my head, and his right hand embraces me!' she is perhaps describing him enclosing her in his arms and anticipating their becoming one flesh.

The Bride clearly loves the King and longs for him. He has made her safe, he has provided for her, and later in the chapter we will see how he wooed her. Here, however, in Song 2:7, the Bride issues what appears to be a warning of sorts. She says:

> 'I adjure you, O daughters of Jerusalem,
> by the gazelles or the does of the field,
> that you not stir up or awaken love until it pleases.'

The Bride is, as it were, seeking to extract an oath from the daughters of Jerusalem. She wants them to swear by what she says here. She charges them 'by the gazelles or the does of the field.' Throughout the Song the Bride will liken her beloved to 'a gazelle or a young stag' (cf. 2:9, 17), so it may be that the Bride means for this adjuration by the gazelles to be taken, in part, as an adjuration to the daughters of Jerusalem by the fact that there are young men whom they, too, will wed. This might be supported by the fact that Solomon elsewhere likens a wife to a doe (Prov. 5:19). Perhaps the charge has the characteristics of the animals in view—the gazelle known for sure-footed swiftness, the doe for grace and beauty. The charge could thus urge the daughters of Jerusalem to be swift in fleeing temptation that they might preserve their attractiveness. It may be significant that the daughters of Jerusalem are charged *by animals*, animals over whom man and woman are given dominion in Genesis 1–2, animals who are not characterized by human dignity. So the Bride may be calling the daughters of Jerusalem to remember that they are humans, given dominion over the animals, that they are not to act the way the beasts do but wait until marriage (cf. Exod. 22:16-17).

The Bride charges the daughters of Jerusalem not to 'stir up or awaken love until it pleases' (Song 2:7). The stirring and awakening of love describes the kinds of emotional and physical behaviors that culminate in the consummation of the marital union. The Bride wants the daughters to defer these activities, not forgo them altogether. And the Bride wants them to defer the gratification of desire because she wants love to be enjoyed to the full. When the Bride says love should not be stirred up 'until it pleases,' the 'it' refers back to love. Here again there are multiple layers of meaning. At one level, 'love pleases' in the sense that love gives pleasure. God has designed physical love for it to give pleasure in marriage. Outside of marriage, prior to marriage in this instance, love may give pleasure, but it comes with shame, fear, guilt, and regret. Within marriage, love will please. Love gives pleasure in marriage, and so the Bride can be taken to say, 'Don't stir up and awaken love until you will be pleased by it.' There might also be a personification of love here, so that love itself will be honored and pleased by those who indulge in it in its appropriate context, in marriage.

People who believe what the Bible teaches about sexuality are sometimes viewed as killjoys, as those who won't let others have any fun. That's not it at all! We want people to have the *most pleasure* with the *least regret*. We want people to be more than beasts, more than dogs or donkeys. We want people to have more than physical trysts that cheapen, demean, and dehumanize. We want people to enjoy the comprehensive interpersonal union of soul and body in the exclusive, permanent, monogamous, life-producing covenant of marriage.[1]

Song 2:8-17: The Song of Spring
Having described her delight in the protection and provision of the King (Song 2:1-3), spoken of his public demonstration of courtesy and love for her (2:4-6), and charged the daughters of Jerusalem to wait for marriage to indulge their passions (2:7), in Song 2:8-17 the Bride describes how the King wooed her to himself. This passage is one of the loveliest poems in all of the world's literature.

The Bride responds to the King's arrival in 2:8-9, recounts his words to her in 2:10-14, and then it is difficult to know whether he or she is speaking in 2:15, but she speaks again of her longing for the King in 2:16-17.

When she responds to his arrival in 2:8-9 there is again a barrier between them. In Song of Songs 1, the barrier to

---

1. This langauge comes from the definition of marriage set forth in Sherif Girgis, Robert George, and Ryan T. Anderson, 'What Is Marriage?,' *Harvard Journal of Law and Public Policy* 34 (2010): 245-87.

intimacy was the Bride's perception of her darkness and concern for her reputation, a barrier overcome by the King's words to her. Now in Song 2:8-9 the barrier is a physical one, and the King comes 'leaping over the mountains, bounding over the hills' to stand at the 'wall' that separates them. Once again, the King's words will overcome the barrier.

The Bride presents the King invoking the universal freshness of spring, the season of love, in 2:10-13. The call in 2:10 is repeated at the end of 2:13, 'Arise, my love, my beautiful one, and come away.' In the impressionistic narrative unfolding across this Song, this invitation can be understood as a request for her hand in marriage. Between these two statements is a description of the new life in a well-watered land, flowers, birds, fruit trees, vines, all fragrant with God's glory. The King concludes with a plea for face-to-face conversation in 2:14. He wants to escape into the countryside to see her face and hear her voice.

Whether the King or the Bride is speaking in Song 2:15, the speaker says:

> Catch the foxes for us, the little foxes
> that spoil the vineyards, for our vineyards are in blossom.

Rather than allow foxes into the blooming vineyard to eat the budding fruit and dig up the fertile soil, the speaker calls for the foxes to be caught so that the vineyard can flourish. The figurative foxes referred to in 2:15 appear to be the kinds of things that happen in a relationship, depicted here as a vineyard, that cause budding love to be ruined, rain-soaked soil to be spoiled. Foxes dig up vines, eat buds, and trample down supports. It seems that just as the keepers of a vineyard need to go through and catch the foxes, the keepers of a relationship need to go through and catch the nuisances. Because of the way the King wants to hear the Bride's voice in 2:14, Solomon appears to suggest that the way to catch these foxes is for King and Bride to talk to one another. They must make sure they understand one another and stay in constant awareness of how they each are doing.

The Bride has related how the King made her feel protected and provided for in 2:1-3, she has recounted his public courtesy expressing his love in 2:4-6, she has charged the daughters to wait for marriage in 2:7, and she has described how the King overcame the wall between them by his wooing words in 2:8-14, even to the point of conversing to catch foxes in 2:15. The King's commitment to protect, provide, woo, and converse bears fruit in what the Bride says in 2:16:

> My beloved is mine, and I am his;
> he grazes among the lilies.

The idea of him grazing picks up the way she likened him to a gazelle in 2:8-9 and will do so again in 2:17. The idea of him grazing among the lilies also recalls the way she likened herself to a lily in 2:1. She was protected and provided for by the fruit tree back in 2:3, and now he is delighted and provided for by the lilies in 2:16.

Most animals are not allowed to graze among flowers. Grazing in the pasture is one thing, but the flowers are to be protected. For the King to be celebrated as grazing among the lilies suggests that the flowers are so abundant that no one is bothered by him grazing there. This would appear to suggest that the King has cultivated a land so rich and abundant and fertile, so like Eden, that he can be celebrated as grazing among the lilies. The imagery of the king from Judah tying his colt to the choice vine in Genesis 49:11 celebrates similar abundance—the colt will eat that vine, but it doesn't appear to matter because choice vines are so plentiful they can be treated as provender.

There is an overtone of 'the cool of the day' from Genesis 3:8 when the Bride says in 2:17, 'Until the day breathes and the shadows flee.' That image of the day breathing seems to be a very subtle reference to that glorious moment in the cool of the day when man and woman walked with God in the Garden of Eden. And then she uses a poetic image that once again communicates her longing for the consummation of their relationship: 'turn, my beloved, be like a gazelle or a young stag on cleft mountains' (Song 2:17). This is another one of those statements that insinuates more than the words actually say. English translators may be seeking to capture what the Hebrew suggests with the phrase 'cleft mountains,' a phrase reminiscent of the word 'cleavage.' She has likened him to a gazelle, and now she says she wants the gazelle to demonstrate his sure-footed speed on the places of cleavage. She is articulating a desire for the moment when the marriage will be consummated, when love will be stirred up and awakened.

Brothers, if you want your wife to talk this way to you, let me assure you that your wife wants you to treat her the way the King treats the Bride in the Song. She wants you to protect her, to provide for her, to show her courtesy in public, and to woo her. She wants you to be someone she can trust, someone with whom she will feel safe. May the Lord make our marriages like the one depicted in the Song.

Conclusion

To this point in this study of Song of Songs 2 we have focused almost exclusively on the human dimensions of the love depicted in the poetry of Song of Songs 2. How might this poetry apply to messianic hope and the love between Yahweh and Israel, Christ and the church? At the level of messianic hope, once again, the King depicted typifies the true King of Israel. The Bridegroom will love his Bride in such a way that she will desire ever-deepening intimacy. At the level of the love between God and His people, the King's behavior in this chapter is like an enacted parable of the way that God in Christ loves His people.

There is no better protector or provider than Jesus. Jesus will take those who belong to Him into the banqueting house for the great marriage supper of the Lamb, His marriage supper. We long for the consummation of God's purposes, and we can trust that when the time is right it will be better than it would be if we cut short God's plan. Jesus has come to us, He woos us to Himself with words of Spirit and life (John 6:63), He calls us to come and follow Him, and He wants us to hear and heed His Word so that He and His Father will come and dwell with us, that we might abide in Him (John 14–15). We are His; He is ours, and we will walk with Him in the cool of the day.

QUESTIONS FOR DISCUSSION

1. Some interpreters think that the King and the Bride in the Song of Songs consummate the relationship in every chapter of the book. Would you agree or disagree with that suggestion? Consider the mention of a wedding day in 3:11 and then what seems to be a moment of unparalleled intimacy in 4:16–5:1. How do these passages affect your understanding of this question?

2. Are you able to identify aspects of your character or behavior that keep your relationship from sounding like the interaction between the King and the Bride in Song of Songs 2? If you are single, how should this question inform your thinking about how you might conduct yourself in a relationship?

3. Consider the adjuration in Song of Songs 2:7. Why do you think the adjuration not to 'stir up or awaken love until it pleases' is made 'by the gazelles or the does of the field'?

4. Are there ways that the adjuration not to stir up love until it pleases needs to be applied to your life? To what you do or say? To what you put before your eyes? To the way you dress?

5. Consider the imagery of the season of spring in Song of Songs 2:10-13. Why do you suppose spring imagery is so often associated with the beginning of love?

4

Like Columns of Smoke from the Wilderness
(Song of Songs 3)

In *The Count of Monte Cristo*, Edmond Dantès suffers terribly in prison for fourteen years. Those years of suffering, however, are also years of a tremendous education from his fellow prisoner, the Abbé Faria. Dantès escapes from prison in a death and resurrection involving substitution. Faria dies, and Dantès takes his place in the body bag, which is dumped in the sea, from which death Dantès rises to visit justice on those who had him wrongly imprisoned. Along the way, Dantès buys out of slavery a princess whom he will later marry, and when he enters into the society to which he brings justice, he enters like a mysterious ruler from some Eastern land. He enters Paris like a column of smoke coming up from the wilderness.

It's a fabulous story, and it appeals to us because Dantès is able to bring off such a satisfying resolution to the injustice and intrigue that brought about his own suffering. He himself not only goes through a kind of death and resurrection enabling him to work retribution for foes and deliverance for friends, he also (figuratively speaking) raises the bride-to-be of an adoptive son from the dead. His resurrection enables, in a sense, the resurrection of his son's bride.

Throughout the story, Dantès is in entire control of the unfolding events. He plans, enacts, and directs like a conductor in full control of his orchestra. He judges the guilty, forgives the repentant, and saves the poor and needy.

Need

Wouldn't it be great to have someone like Edmond Dantès on our side? Don't you wish you had someone who could do justice, grant forgiveness, and work salvation for people with whom you sympathize?

The plot of *The Count of Monte Cristo* and its resolution resonate with us because it subtly imitates the plot of the true story of the world. There is a better hero than Edmond Dantès in a bigger plot than the one written by Alexandre Dumas.

Main Point

In Song of Songs 3 we see King Solomon coming to his wedding, answering the eager longings of the Bride. The description of the scene points backward, calling to mind the way Yahweh came to Israel's rescue at the exodus, which also points forward, to the fulfillment of our longings at the marriage feast of the Lamb.

Context

We have seen the King give the Bride confidence and standing by his words in Song 1, and their mutual love makes their home into a garden bough. Then in chapter 2 we saw the King come leaping over the mountains, bounding over the hills to sing the song of spring, calling the Bride to come away with him. Now in chapter 3 we read of her longing and him arriving for the wedding feast.

Preview

Song 3:1-5, The Bride's Longing

Song 3:6-11, The King's Arrival

Song 3:1-5: The Bride's Longing

In Song 3:1 the Bride is depicted saying, 'On my bed by night I sought him whom my soul loves; I sought him but found him not.' We could render the first phrase of Song of Songs 3:1, 'On my bed in the nights.' Two things to point out here: first, the Bride is speaking of *her* bed, not *their* bed. It is of course possible that the King did not necessarily sleep in the same bed with his wife, but throughout verses 1-4 it appears that the King and the Bride are not even in the same house, which adds to the impression that they have not yet married and will not consummate the relationship until 4:16–5:1. Second, the phrase rendered in the ESV 'by night' could just as easily be translated 'in the nights,' and that raises the question of what kind of account we find in the first four verses of Song 3.

Some conclude that the Bride here is describing a dream that she had, and this is reflected in the ESV's subtitle over 3:1-5, 'The Bride's Dream.' We do not need to be that specific about the kind of experience the Bride is depicted describing here. Once again, this is a poem, not a historical narrative, and in poetry we are not dealing with a precisely delineated account of exactly what happened. Rather, the poet has created a scene in which the Bride speaks of her longing for the King. The uncertainty of the circumstances does not take away from the certainty of the sentiments being communicated. So what we read here in Song 3:1-4 *definitely* communicates the Bride's longing for the King.

It is a kind of archetypal image to have the single person, in this case the Bride-to-be, lying in bed by night pining for her beloved. That is what is being depicted here, and the dreamlike quality of the description captures the essence of what it is to long for the companionship of marriage.

She recounted how the King came to her in 2:8-9, sang to her the song of spring in 2:10-15, and concluded with statements communicating her longing for consummation in 2:16-17. Now between the King asking for her hand in marriage with the proposal to 'Arise ... and come away' (2:10, 13) and the wedding day in 3:6-11, the Bride describes how she spent the nights between betrothal and consummation longing for her beloved.[1]

She relates twice in verse 1 and once in verse 2 that she 'sought' the King. In verse 1 the seeking is done on her bed in the nights, and she states that on her bed she found him not. This leads naturally to what she says in 3:2:

> I will rise now and go about the city, in the streets and in the squares;

---

1. So Estes in Fredericks and Estes, *Ecclesiastes and the Song of Songs*, 335.

I will seek him whom my soul loves.
I sought him, but found him not.

She sought him in the nights on her bed and did not find him, so she went through the streets and squares of the city but didn't find him there either. Verses 1 and 2 of Song of Songs 3 end with the exact same phrase, 'I sought him, but found him not.' The repetition of this phrase stresses the Bride's earnest, persistent longing for her beloved.

Note that once again there is separation between the Bride and the King. Whereas in chapters 1 and 2, the separation was overcome by words the King spoke, here the Bride is *seeking* the King. It's not hard to figure out what's going on at the level of human love here, is it? Married people, do you remember what it felt like to be engaged? To long for the consummation of the betrothal? Single people, I know that many of you can identify with what the Bride feels here. This is good and right. It's a good thing to want to be married. God Himself said it wasn't good for man to be alone (Gen. 2:18). Be encouraged by the way things work out for the Bride. This passage isn't guaranteeing that your desires for human love will be realized, but there is a deeper meaning to this love that will be fulfilled. More on that shortly.

In Song 3:3 the Bride encounters the watchmen. These seem to be official keepers of the peace in the city to oversee and serve as lookouts. There is a similar night encounter with them in 5:7, and there might be a subtle hint of them in 8:1.

No sooner has she moved on from the watchmen than she finds the beloved in 3:4. By way of observation, the word 'found' occurs in verses 1, 2, 3, and 4. In verses 1 and 2, she 'found him not.' Then in verse 3 the watchmen found her. Then in verse 4, she found the beloved. It seems that the Bride's action of bringing the King into the chamber of her mother is connected to the celebrations of the wedding (cf. Gen. 24:67, where Isaac brought Rebekah into Sarah's tent, 'and she became his wife'). The Bride taking him into her mother's house may have been a component of the week-long wedding celebrations we read of elsewhere in the Old Testament (cf. Gen. 29:27; Judg. 14:12).

Before we look again at the admonition the poet has put on the lips of the Bride in 3:5, ponder the pattern that has unfolded to this point in the book. In Song 1, the Bride was concerned about her appearance and standing, and the King's words gave her confidence in herself and access to himself. In Song 2, a wall separated the Bride from the King, and the King came and invited her to arise and go away with him. Now in Song 3 she sought him on her bed by night, rose to search for him, was found by the watchmen, then found the King and took him to her mother's chamber.

What follows in 3:6-11 looks like a wedding procession, but before we examine 3:6-11, let's consider the light it sheds on 3:1-4. Solomon as author is about to present the Bride describing the idealized Solomon of the Song (the character in the poem, not the historical person) coming up from the wilderness in terms reminiscent of the exodus from Egypt. Solomon clearly means to remind his audience of the exodus from Egypt in Song of Song 3:6-11, and this implies that the King's wedding to his Bride was meant to call to mind the Sinai Covenant, with Solomon representing Yahweh and the Bride representing Israel. The correspondences are impressionistic, not exact, and the details are not necessarily to be pressed. Nevertheless, Solomon poetically evokes the exodus and the tabernacle, as we will see when we consider the relevant statements. How does 3:6-11 inform 3:1-4?

Song of Songs 3:1-4 depicts a young lady frantic to find her betrothed. In each of these four verses she refers to him as 'him whom my soul loves' (Song 3:1, 2, 3, 4). Verse 1 has her restless on her bed seeking and not finding him, verse 2 has her going through the streets and squares of the city seeking and not finding him, verse 3 has the watchmen finding her and she asks them if they have seen him, and all the repetition of the seeking and not finding builds tension, heightens drama.

There is another poem in the Bible where the speaker is seeking, yearning, in bed at night. David, Solomon's father, wrote of his longing for God in Psalm 63:1-6 (italics added to highlight correspondences with Song 3:1-4):[2]

---

2. While the Hebrew terms for 'seek' and 'bed' are not the same in Psalm 63 and Song 3:1-4, the concepts are clearly synonymous.

O God, you are my God; earnestly *I seek you*;
my soul thirsts for you, my flesh faints for you, as in a dry and
    weary land where there is no water.
So I have looked upon you in the sanctuary, beholding your
    power and glory.
Because your steadfast love is better than life, my lips will
    praise you.
So I will bless you as long as I live;
in your name I will lift up my hands.
My soul will be satisfied as with fat and rich food,
and my mouth will praise you with joyful lips,
when I remember you *upon my bed*,
and meditate on you *in the watches of the night*;

In Psalm 63:7 David uses an image familiar from Ruth's request to Boaz as she asked him to be her kinsman redeemer and make her his wife: 'Spread your wings over your servant' (Ruth 3:9). David applies this image to his relationship with the Lord when he writes in Psalm 63:7, 'in the shadow of your wings I will sing for joy.' The Hebrew verb David uses in Psalm 63:8, 'My soul *clings* to you,' is the same verb used in Genesis 2:24, 'Therefore a man shall leave ... and *hold fast* to his wife' (italics mine). The point here is that when David speaks of his longing for the Lord to come and establish the promises of the covenant He made with him, he employs metaphors with roots in the covenant of marriage.

In Song of Songs 3:1-4, Solomon has dramatized the same longing that David articulated for the Lord. Solomon depicts the Bride yearning for the King in the same way that David yearned for the Lord. Solomon means to add fuel to the fire. He intends to fan the flames of longing and devotion.

The more you want something, the longer you have to wait for it, the more satisfying is the realization of your anticipation. If you have waited in purity, postponement intensifies the fulfillment of desire. If you have been faithful, if you have earnestly desired, when your relief comes you will know the truth of Proverbs 13:12, 'desire fulfilled is a tree of life.'

The building tension of Song of Songs 3:1-3 sets up the Bride's passionate embrace of the King in 3:4. Solomon understands the innermost meaning of marriage, and he uses this relationship he depicts between the King and the Bride to personalize the relationship between Yahweh and His people.

Is there a correspondence between the history of Yahweh's relationship with Israel and the impressionistic drama sung in the Song? If the wedding procession in 3:6-11 corresponds to the exodus from Egypt, then perhaps the Bride's longing in 3:1-4 corresponds to Israel in Egypt longing for salvation. The Bride yearned for and sought the King in 3:1-2, then was found by the watchmen in 3:3 (perhaps a subtle reminiscence of Moses their prophet and intercessor?).[3] Then the Bride found the King, and the initial events of the wedding were set in motion with her taking the King to her mother's house in 3:4.

The spiritual correspondence with Yahweh and Israel takes nothing away from the reality of human love in Song of Songs 3:1-4. There really is a depiction of the human Bride-to-be longing for her betrothed, the King. With the Bible's broader use of marital concepts deriving from God's relationship with His people, and with the exodus imagery in 3:6-11, it seems Solomon also intended to tie the human longing of the Bride to the way God's people were to yearn for Him, as they did when they languished in Egypt.

There is hope here for singles, even those who will never marry. It is good and right to long for the kind of companionship and intimacy only possible within the one-flesh covenant of man and wife in marriage. And even if the Lord never gives you that blessing, the longing will find its ultimate fulfillment in something that—if you trust Christ—He will give you. The longing for a spouse is a shadow of the longing for the Lord's salvation, the longing for Him to save His people and dwell with them face to face. Even if the Lord never gives you a wife or a husband in this life, if you trust in Jesus, He will save you, and you will dwell with Him forever, and the longing of your heart will be realized. You will be His bride, and He will be your incomparable bridegroom.

---

3. If the Bride seeking the King in Song 3:1-4 corresponds to Israel crying out to Yahweh in Exodus 2:23-25, then the Bride's second night search and encounter with the watchmen (after she rejected the King) in 5:2-8 can be seen to correspond to what Solomon knows Israel will do (cf. 1 Kings 8:46-53): reject Yahweh, be exiled from his presence, then seek him from exile and be restored (cf. Deut. 4:25-31).

The Bride once again admonishes the audience of the Song to wait patiently for the right time and the right way for the satisfaction of love in Song 3:5 (see comments on 2:7). We can neither bring in the Kingdom nor cause a spouse to appear for us and a wedding to happen until the Lord's appointed times for those consummations. We must wait on Him, and we must look to Him for our joy and satisfaction until that day comes.

Song 3:6-11: The King's Arrival

The evidence for thinking that Solomon the poet caused the character of the Bride in the Song to describe the King in terms that are reminiscent of the exodus from Egypt is found in what the Bride says in 3:6-11. She begins in 3:6:

> What is that coming up from the wilderness like columns of
>   smoke,
> perfumed with myrrh and frankincense,
> with all the fragrant powders of a merchant?

The first phrase of the question could be rendered, 'Who is this ...' (so NIV), and the comparison 'like columns of smoke' evokes the pillar of cloud and fire that led Israel through the wilderness (cf. Exod. 13:21), along with the smoke wrapped around Mount Sinai when the Lord came down on the mountain in Exodus 19:18. The word 'columns' is not the word used in Exodus, but Joel uses the word (perhaps under the influence of this passage in the Song?) when he speaks of the way the Lord will provide a new-exodus style deliverance for His people 'afterward' (Joel 2:30, Matt. 3:3; cf. 2:28, Matt. 3:1).

Solomon comes up 'perfumed with myrrh and frank-incense' and with 'all the fragrant powders of a merchant' in Song 3:6. This terminology is used in Exodus 30:22-38 (especially Exod. 30:32, 34). The myrrh is used in the anointing oil prepared for 'the tent of meeting and the ark of the testimony' (30:26), along with the utensils, and Aaron and his sons (30:27-33). The frankincense is used in the incense to be put in the tent of meeting (30:34-38).

The Bride's question from 3:6, 'Who/what is this?' is answered in 3:7-8:

Behold, it is the litter of Solomon!
Around it are sixty mighty men,
some of the mighty men of Israel,
all of them wearing swords and expert in war,
each with his sword at his thigh, against terror by night.

We'll read more about the 'litter' in 3:9-10. Solomon seems to be in a palanquin, which is a covered, boxlike, enclosed vehicle carried on poles that rest on the shoulders of men. A box with curtains is almost like a tent, as though this is Solomon's own personal tabernacle, or ark, carried on poles, coming up like smoke out of the wilderness. Just as the tabernacle was surrounded by the tribes of Israel, described like army regiments, marching as to war when they pulled up camp, so Solomon, who is being carried as the tabernacle and ark were on poles, is surrounded by these crack troops.

This way of looking at Solomon coming up out of the wilderness for his wedding would seem to be supported by what Moses narrates in Numbers 23–24. As Balaam describes the camp of Israel in his attempt to curse Israel for Balak, he says in Numbers 23:21-22:

The LORD their God is with them, and the shout of a king is
    among them.
God brings them out of Egypt and is for them like the horns
    of the wild ox.

Balaam spoke of Yahweh in the midst of Israel like a king, and the reference to Him being like the horns of the wild ox means that Yahweh is their military power. In the Song, Yahweh's earthly representative, Israel's King, also comes up out of the wilderness with military power. In Numbers, Balaam looked at the camp of Israel, with the tabernacle in its midst, and spoke of a king with his martial power.

It seems that in Song of Songs 3:6-11 Solomon invokes this imagery. He depicts the poem-version of himself as the king of Israel who stands for Yahweh and His authority. Solomon's description of the wedding procession recalls Israel coming up out of the wilderness with Yahweh in their midst in the tabernacle, the ark of the covenant being carried on poles, and as Yahweh was to marry Israel at Sinai, so Solomon comes to marry his Bride in Jerusalem.

As Yahweh was surrounded by the tribes of Israel arranged like the regiments of an army, Solomon's sixty mighty men surround his carriage.

The mention of 'mighty men' of Israel in Song 3:7 calls to mind David's mighty men (2 Sam. 23:8-39), but whereas David had thirty mighty men (23:18-19), Solomon has doubled that number with his sixty (Song 3:7). The Bride has nothing to fear from the terrors of night.

The points of contact between Solomon's palanquin and the tabernacle/temple continue in Song of Songs 3:9-10. Solomon got cedars from Lebanon for the building of the temple (1 Kings 5:1-6), and in Song 3:9 the Bride says, 'King Solomon made himself a carriage from the wood of Lebanon.' In Song 3:10 she relates, 'He made its posts of silver, its back of gold, its seat of purple; its interior was inlaid with love by the daughters of Jerusalem.' Silver, gold, and purple are frequently referenced in the instructions for the tabernacle. Nearly everything in it was gold.

Just as Yahweh came out of Egypt, residing in the tabernacle over the mercy seat on the ark of the covenant, borne along by the poles on the shoulders of the priests, preceded by pillar of fire and cloud, Solomon comes up like a column of smoke from the wilderness, in a boxlike, covered, moving tent, carried on poles that rest on the shoulders of those who serve him, surrounded by his special forces, arriving in the city of the great king, Jerusalem, for the consummation of the covenant.

Having spoken of the handiwork of the daughters of Jerusalem in 3:10, the Bride summons the daughters of Zion in 3:11:

> Go out, O daughters of Zion, and look upon King Solomon,
> with the crown with which his mother crowned him on the
> day of his wedding, on the day of the gladness of his heart.

Solomon's mother Bathsheba was instrumental in David keeping his word to make Solomon king (1 Kings 1:11-37). It seems that at this point in the poem we have come to the celebration of the long-anticipated wedding. It also seems that this wedding is presented in terms that are intended by the author of the poem to recall an earlier wedding, the one between Yahweh and Israel, and given Solomon's standing in the line of descent of the seed of the woman (Gen. 3:15), given the promises to David about his offspring, whom the Lord would raise up to build a house for the name of the Lord (2 Sam. 7:12-13), as this wedding points back to the covenant between Yahweh and Israel at Sinai, it also points forward to the one between Christ and the church (cf. Rev. 19:7).

Conclusion

Are you a single person longing for a spouse? Let me encourage you to indulge in a transposition of that longing. Use the emotional energy you feel to long for the day when Christ will come and take his Bride. Stir up the longing the Bride recounts in Song 3:1-4, place the boundary of the admonition in 3:5 around that longing, trusting that in God's good time Christ will come just as He was seen to go, and feast your imagination on the glory of that day. As great as Solomon was, and as impressive as the parade of his palanquin would have been, we await the coming of one greater than Solomon (cf. Matt. 12:42).

Lift up your eyes, church. Your Redemption draweth nigh. Behold, the Bridegroom cometh! Blessed are those who have washed their robes and made them white in the blood of the Lamb, those who will be ready when the marriage of the Lamb has come (cf. Rev. 7:14; 19:7).

A better Savior is coming than the Count of Monte Cristo could ever be. We do well to heed the Count's counsel to his adopted son, Morrel, and the bride he raised from the dead, Valentine, when he wrote them in his parting letter:

> Tell the angel who will watch over your future destiny, Morrel, to pray sometimes for a man, who like Satan thought himself for an instant equal to God, but who now acknowledges with Christian humility that God alone possesses supreme power and infinite wisdom. Perhaps those prayers may soften the remorse he feels in his heart. As for you, Morrel, this is the secret of my conduct towards you. There is neither happiness nor misery in the world; there is only the comparison of one state with another, nothing more. He who has felt the deepest

grief is best able to experience supreme happiness. We must have felt what it is to die, Morrel, that we may appreciate the enjoyments of living.

Live, then, and be happy, beloved children of my heart, and never forget that until the day when God shall deign to reveal the future to man, all human wisdom is summed up in these two words, – 'Wait and hope.'
Your friend,
Edmond Dantès,
Count of Monte Cristo.[4]

Wait and hope, my friends, for he will come.
Like a column of smoke from the wilderness, more fragrant than frankincense,
Comes the one whose presence the Ark of the Covenant represented.
Almighty power to protect, danger of night will be no more.
Better than the temple itself, the King will come to Zion,
Crowned for the day of his wedding, to claim his Bride, clothed in fine white linen.
Ten thousand times ten thousand will throng about him, waving the branches of palm,
Blessed is he who comes in the Name of the Lord.

QUESTIONS FOR DISCUSSION

1. Can you identify with the longing the Bride articulates in Song of Songs 3:1-3?

2. Are you seeking the Lord the way the Bride sought the King?

3. If you are unmarried, how does the admonition of Song of Songs 3:5 apply to you? Can this admonition be applied to spiritual paramours (idols you would put in place of the Lord)?

4. Can you imagine anything more glorious than Israel's wisest and most wealthy king entering Jerusalem on his wedding day? Does your expectation

---

4. Alexandre Dumas, *The Count of Monte Cristo*, cited from http://www.online-literature.com/dumas/cristo/117/.

of Christ's return to consummate the covenant accord with his wealth, power, splendor, and magnificence?

5. Song of Songs 3:11 speaks of the gladness of the King's heart on the day of his wedding. Do you dare to believe that the Lord Jesus will be glad of heart on the day He claims His Bride?

5

The Consummation of the Covenant
(Song of Songs 4)

Cultural norms and expectations have penetrated our thinking in more ways than we have recognized. At so many points we are more conformed than transformed, particularly when it comes to how we think about marital relations.

How do we resist our proclivity to sin and the pervasive celebration of defilement that surrounds us? Where do we go for a different way of thinking about what God intended for intimacy between husband and wife in marriage?

Need
Are you single and tempted to lust? Are you married and finding that lustful attitudes and actions are defiling the marriage bed?

How can we take our thoughts captive to the knowledge of Christ? How can we grow to pray that God would redirect our impulses?

How are we to think about marital relations? Does the Bible have anything to say about these matters? Does Song of Songs 4?

Main Point
In Song of Songs 4 Solomon depicts himself speaking to his beloved as though she is the land of promise, the Garden of

Eden, teeming with life, flowing with milk and honey, and the consummation of their covenant comes when he enters the garden where living water flows.

Context
In Song of Songs 1 the Bride was insecure about her appearance and her place in society, and the King's words addressed both of those problems. In Song 2 there was a wall that separated the Bride from the King, and the King summoned the Bride to come away with him. In Song 3 she sought the King, encountered the watchmen, then found the King. The King then came up from the wilderness like a cloud of smoke, borne aloft in a covered, tent-like box made of wood from Lebanon, carried on poles that rest on shoulders, entering Jerusalem for his wedding. The whole scene is reminiscent of Yahweh leading Israel up from Egypt through the wilderness with the pillar of fire and cloud that the people might enjoy covenant with Him in the land.

In the unfolding impressionistic narrative of the Song of Songs, the wedding day has come (Song 3:11), and in Song 4 the King celebrates the Bride's beauty as the covenant is consummated. The way that Solomon portrays the King describing the Bride teaches us how to think about God's good gift of intimacy in marriage.

Preview

> 4:1-7, Flowing with Milk and Honey
>
> 4:8-15, Living Water in the Garden
>
> 4:16–5:1, Consummation

Song 4:1-7: Flowing with Milk and Honey
Song 3:6-11 depicted the King making his way up from the wilderness into Jerusalem in solemn procession, and 3:11 calls the Daughters of Zion to go out and look at Solomon 'on the day of his wedding.' It seems that in 4:1–5:1 we have a poetic rehearsal of the King's response to his Bride on the wedding day.

Though I am referring to the female character in the Song as 'the Bride' throughout this study, it is worth noting that the only occurrences of that word, 'Bride,' in the Song are all found between 4:8 and 5:1. She is not referred to as 'Bride' before or after this passage. In Song 4:1-7 the King will extol the beauty of the Bride using imagery that resonates most deeply with him, imagery that describes the promised land. Then he will invite the Bride to come with him and describe her as a locked garden in 4:8-15, before the consummation of the marriage in 4:16–5:1.

Many interpreters today seek to exposit how the descriptions in Song 4:1-15 capture the physical appearance of the Bride. Solomon is describing his delight in the Bride's physical appearance in this passage, but I don't think the point of comparing her hair, for instance, to a flock of goats in 4:1 is to suggest that it is dark and wavy. That is, I don't think Solomon intends for the imagery he uses to extol the Bride's appearance to describe her physical appearance. Rather, this imagery is meant to communicate *what she means to him*, and to communicate that he has chosen imagery that is biblically and theologically profound.

Let me summarize the comparisons in Song 4:1-6: In verse 1 he compares her eyes to doves and her hair to a flock of goats. In verse 2 her teeth are likened to clean, shorn, fertile sheep. In verse 3 her lips are like a scarlet thread, and the only other place that phrase ('scarlet thread') is used in the Bible is in the account of the deliverance of Rahab at the fall of Jericho (Josh. 2:18). Then also in verse 3 her cheeks, or perhaps her temples, are likened to 'halves of a pomegranate,' fruit.

In these comparisons in Song 4:1-3, then, we have birds, goats, sheep (bearing twins), an allusion to the conquest of the land under Joshua, then fruit. The King is describing the Bride as a land that is bursting with living creatures and fruit. In Song 4:4 he likens her neck to the tower of David and references the shields of warriors. The point is not that there is some correspondence between her jewelry and the rows of stones used to build that tower. No, the point is to liken her to the land of promise, protected by the Davidic King. In order to think together about what the imagery means, let's work back through the comparisons in more detail.

In Song 4:1 the King says to her, 'Behold, you are beautiful, my love, behold, you are beautiful! Your eyes are doves behind your veil. Your hair is like a flock of goats leaping down the slopes of Gilead.' If you were going to elaborate on the idea that your beloved is beautiful, what imagery would you use? The imagery that Solomon has chosen to use is imagery of a land sustaining life. There are birds and animals because the land is fertile not barren. This imagery is reminiscent of the Bible's depictions of the way that God will bless the land of Israel if they will keep the covenant (cf. Deut. 28:1-14). Solomon begins with her head: eyes and hair in verse 1, teeth in verse 2, lips and either temples or cheeks in verse 3, then he moves downward to her neck in verse 4 and her chest in verse 5.

He describes her eyes as doves in Song 4:1. With all the land imagery in this passage, perhaps this comparison is meant to recall the dove that Noah sent out from the ark after seven days to see if the waters had receded from the new creation after the flood (Gen. 8:8-12). Noah then left the ark as a new Adam (Gen. 9:1, 7) entering into a new covenant (9:9, 11) in a new creation (cf. 1:2, 9 and 8:1-2).

There is more to the King comparing her hair to a flock of goats in Song 4:1 than an attempt to describe its color or waviness or length. This is the Song of Songs, the most sublime Song, the pinnacle of Solomon's artistic production as a poet, and this passage is building toward the climactic moment in the Song when the King will enter the sacred garden, where he enjoys shameless nakedness with his Bride, for covenantal consummation.

In this passage Solomon uses the language of what matters most to him, language that describes the land God promised to His people, language that depicts God's blessing on that land if and when God's people keep God's law. In short, Solomon is using the language that is used elsewhere in the Old Testament for the Kingdom of God, and he is comparing his beloved to the blessed land.

Deuteronomy 28 describes the blessings the people will enjoy if they will keep the Torah (Deut. 28:1-3), and in 28:4 we read, 'Blessed shall be the fruit of your womb and the fruit of your ground and the fruit of your cattle, the increase of your herds and the young of your flock.' Solomon depicts this poetically in Song 4:2: 'Your teeth are like a flock of shorn ewes that have come up from the washing, all of which bear twins, and not one among them has lost its young.' This does not for a second deny that the King's Bride was beautiful, that she wasn't missing any teeth, but I think there's more to it than that. This idea that the sheep bear twins and do not miscarry points to God's blessing, as articulated in Deuteronomy 28:4 (cf. Exod. 23:26, 'None shall miscarry or be barren in your land').

With the imagery going in this direction, it would fit for Solomon to allude to the story of the capture of Jericho and the deliverance of Rahab by the sign of the scarlet thread in Song 4:3, 'Your lips are like a scarlet thread.' According to Ruth 4:18-22 and Matthew 1:5-6, Rahab was Solomon's great, great, great-grandmother. In a passage depicting the glory of God's purpose for human relations, for the joy of the redeemed, how fitting that there would be an allusion to the mercy God showed to Rahab, rescued from a life of harlotry, married, mother in the line of the Messiah. The reference to the scarlet thread evokes Rahab, and it adds an overtone of the conquest of the land.

Solomon suggests that just as Israel inhabited the land God had prepared for them, so he is now taking possession of the Bride that God has prepared for him. She is lovely to him, as he says in the next line of verse 3, 'your mouth is lovely,' and she is to him like the fruit of the land, 'Your cheeks are like halves of a pomegranate behind your veil.'

So the Bride is like the land, and this is a land that has a protector. This is a land that, like the Garden of Eden, is being worked and kept (cf. Gen. 2:15). Solomon's depiction of the land in these terms may have influenced Isaiah 5, where Isaiah sings a love song for his beloved, describing Yahweh planting a garden and building a watchtower in it (Isa. 5:1-2). In fact, the only use of the term 'beloved' (דודי, *dodi*) outside the Song of Songs is in Isaiah 5:1.[1] Isaiah uses a term from the Song, uses imagery reminiscent of the Song, and in Isaiah's account Yahweh plays the role the King plays in the Song.

---

1. A similar form, with slightly different vowel pointing, is used in 1 Chronicles 27:4, but it appears to be a proper name.

This could be an instance of an Old Testament author, Isaiah, interpreting the Song of Songs as having reference to the relationship between God and Israel.

When Solomon presents the King saying to the Bride, 'Your neck is like the tower of David, built in rows of stones; on it hang a thousand shields, all of them shields of warriors,' he describes her with language that says she is protected. The royal power of the Davidic King ensures her safety. In this poetry, the King declares to his Bride that to him she is the land of promise, that she is protected as by the tower of David, arrayed with shields to guard and keep.

Solomon has described her head and neck in Song 4:1-4, and he uses delicate and sacred imagery to speak of her chest in 4:5: 'Your two breasts are like two fawns, twins of a gazelle, that graze among the lilies.' Solomon uses similar imagery of 'a lovely deer, a graceful doe' for a wife in Proverbs 5:19, and the next words are 'Let her breasts fill you at all times with delight.' Again, the image uses elegant, graceful creatures to describe a tender loveliness, and since the Bride's breasts will be the source of life for their children, so these healthy fawns connect the fruitfulness of land and Bride (cf. the opposite in Hosea 9:14, 'a miscarrying womb and dry breasts').

The King of Israel celebrates his Bride's beauty, describing her in imagery that communicates what means most to him: the land of promise under the covenant blessings of God. What would be connoted by his comparison of her breasts to 'two fawns, twins of a gazelle, that graze among the lilies' (Song 4:5)?[2] As with 2:17, the image of a gazelle grazing among lilies communicates the animal enjoying not just roughage in the pasture but flowers. Likening her breasts to twins born of a gazelle that grazes among the lilies communicates

---

2. The Bride referred to the King grazing among the lilies in Song 2:17, and she will describe him doing so again in 6:3. This word 'lilies' actually isn't used all that many times in the Hebrew Bible. The two large Bronze pillars in the temple, Jachin and Boaz, were adorned with capitals that were made to look like lilies (1 Kings 7:19, 22), as was the brim of the bronze sea at the temple (7:26). There are thematic connections between Eden, tabernacle, temple, and the land of promise. The term rendered 'grazes' is the same term that with another subject would be rendered 'shepherds,' so when used of Solomon in 6:3, the phrase could connote something like: he shepherds among the lily-worked pillars at the temple. Used here of the Bride, the reference to lilies among which she grazes might communicate that she, too, spends time at the temple because of her relationship with the King.

awareness of privilege. The use of the term 'gazelle' here is significant. A homonym is a word that sounds, and may be spelled, the same as another word but carries a different meaning. In Hebrew, the term צבי (*tsevi*), can mean *gazelle* or *beauty*. Solomon uses the feminine form here, צביה (*tseviyah*), but those who attend to wordplays and poetic devices can hear the suggestion that the two breasts of the Bride have been likened to twin daughters of beauty, who graze among lilies.

In Song of Songs 4:6 Solomon uses a phrase that the Bride used in 2:17, 'Until the day breathes and the shadows flee,' and as there it seems to invoke here the 'cool of the day' in the Garden of Eden when God walked with Adam and Eve. Here in 4:6 Solomon says, 'I will go away to the mountain of myrrh and the hill of frankincense.' This is not an indication that Solomon is leaving his beloved for another place but a metaphorical statement about where he is going. Because myrrh and frankincense were used in the special anointing oil and incense made for the tabernacle (Exod. 30:22-23, 34), and because the Garden of Eden is spoken of as a 'holy mountain' in Ezekiel 28:14, I would suggest that Solomon is referring to his intention to consummate the marriage, and he describes it as entering the temple in terms that pick up the way the tabernacle and temple symbolized Eden. We're about to see a lot more about Eden in Song 4:12-15.

The connotations of Eden and the temple lend a sacred shade to this light. Her body is holy. Like the Garden and the temple, the body of the Bride is sacred space only enjoyed by those authorized to do so. When we talk about this book, we should think and speak of the body of the Bride in the Song with the reverence and decorum Solomon uses. That same reverence and decorum is due to the bodies of all women.

Solomon then repeats in Song 4:7 the language of 4:1, and the repetition of the same terms creates a bookend, an *inclusio* marking the conclusion of the King's speech, which has been addressed directly to the Bride. He has been speaking to her of what she is to him. He says to her in 4:7, 'You are altogether beautiful, my love; there is no flaw in you.' The King's words overcame the barriers to intimacy in Song 1 and 2, then she sought him in Song 3, and now she is, to use the language of

Ephesians 5:27, 'without spot or wrinkle or any such thing ... holy and without blemish.'

There is a parallel here, a type, of the way that Jesus overcomes the barriers to intimacy between Himself and His Bride, the church. Jesus has paid the penalty for our sin and spoken words that summon us to Himself. We who seek Him will be holy, without flaw, because of what Jesus has done.

The words Solomon placed on the lips of the Bride in Song 3:6-11 served to identify the King with Yahweh, coming out of Egypt, entering Jerusalem. Now Solomon has the King addressing the Bride as though she is the land of promise in 4:1-7. Just as Solomon and his Bride will dwell together as man and wife, Yahweh made a covenant with Israel that He might dwell among them in the land of promise. Solomon, son of David, King in Jerusalem, celebrates the glory of his Bride and extols her beauty. He does so in a way that points *both* to the deeper, religious significance of marriage as a picture of the covenant between God and His people *and* to the role of the Son of David in consummating the purposes of God.

The color palette of language and conceptual imagery Solomon poetically employed to paint this most intimate moment between the King and the Bride in the Song is mixed of the most important realities in the world to him. What mattered more to Solomon, in spite of his sin and failures, than God and God's purposes to establish His Kingdom? What could Solomon have imagined being better than dwelling in God's place as God's people under God's law and enjoying God's blessing? Solomon used this imagery to give living color to the goodness of the wedding of the Bride and the King and its consummation.

When you think of human sexuality and marriage, do you think the way Solomon does? If you were to address your bride to describe her beauty, would you have to get your thoughts out of the gutter, or at least out of the ruts of the culture? Would you use images that evoked the new creation Noah was delivered through the ark to enjoy (doves), the blessing of God manifested in fields that can support birds and flocks that don't miscarry, the work of God to give His people the land when He defeated Jericho (scarlet thread), and would you speak of the work of a new Adam who is guarding the new garden (tower of David)? Would your description of the marriage bed sound like a trip to the temple to walk with God in the cool of the day, like a newly opened path into the Garden of Eden?

May the Lord deliver us from the filth of our culture, from the ways of thinking and talking that should not even be named among us (Eph. 5:3). Pray for the Lord to renew your mind. Fight to drive the world's lingo and behaviors out of your mind when they seek to take you captive. Take your thoughts captive to Christ. Don't think about your wife's beauty, her sacred spaces, in fleshly ways. Marriage is about Christ and the church. Let's think about it that way. Let's think and talk about marriage as though it corresponds to what matters most to us, which it does! Don't defile it. Don't profane it. Don't be like Nadab and Abihu provoking God's wrath at the holy place (Lev. 10:1-2). Marriage corresponds to the way that God has worked to redeem His people and covenant with them in Christ. Let's think about the beauty of our wives in terms of the glorious things that God has done for us.

If I were to adapt Solomon's way of speaking to new-covenant realities and use this language to speak to my wife today, I might say something like this:

> Your face is a visible expression to me of the blessing of God.
> Seeing you I'm reminded that I'm redeemed and given life I don't deserve.
> Nothing matters more to me than Jesus and His Kingdom, and by God's grace our marriage enacts these most important things in the world.
> Gazing on your beauty is like looking out from the pulpit at a church full of people hungry for the Word of God, crying out, 'Keep preaching!'
> Our union is like a trip into the new Jerusalem, where righteousness dwells.

Song 4:8-15: Living Water in the Garden

Having described the significance of her appearance to him in Song 4:1-7, the King is now presented inviting the Bride to come with him. For the first time the King will address her as 'my bride' in 4:8, and he will use that word to describe her five more times in this context (4:9, 10, 11, 12; 5:1). It seems from 4:9 that the King and the Bride are eye to eye, and he will describe her as being like the Garden of Eden and the land of promise in 4:11–5:1. The King, the character Solomon in the poem, has been crowned on the day of his wedding (3:11), described the bride's beauty in 4:1-7, and he will invite her to go with him into the promised land, the new Eden, in 4:8-15.

Solomon presents the King saying in Song 4:8: 'Come with me from Lebanon, my bride; come with me from Lebanon. Depart from the peak of Amana, from the peak of Senir and Hermon, from the dens of lions, from the mountains of leopards.' The place names here, Lebanon, Senir, Hermon, are all in Lebanon, which is to the north of Israel. So Solomon has come up from the wilderness, like Israel with the tabernacle, and now he summons the Bride down from Lebanon, like the cedars for the temple.

It seems that the King and the Bride are eye to eye in Song 4:9: 'You have captivated my heart, my sister, my bride; you have captivated my heart with one glance of your eyes, with one jewel of your necklace.' The phrase 'captivated my heart' could be rendered 'enheartened,' as in 'encouraged,' or it could refer to his heart beating more rapidly. The point is obvious. He is euphoric over her. With this, the King refers to her as 'my sister, my bride.'

I am not exactly sure of all the cultural connotations of marriage in Ancient Israel.[3] The Bride's comments in 8:1 indicate that she wishes he had been her brother, but that seems to be a statement communicating her passion for him, her desire to kiss him in public without reproach, so it's not quite the same as married people being regarded as brother-sister, which is what the King calling her 'my sister, my bride' might indicate in 4:9, 10, 12, and 5:1. The celebration of the King's 'name' in Song 1:3 was reminiscent of the blessing of Abraham, where God promised to make his name great (Gen. 12:2). Similarly, when Solomon presents the King calling his beloved 'my sister, my bride,' he may mean to evoke Genesis 20:12 in the minds of his audience, where we read that Abraham and Sarah had the same father though a different mother. These sister-bride references could thus

---

3. In the inter-testamental, apocryphal book of Tobit, husbands and wives are also spoken of as brothers and sisters. See Tobit 7:11, 15; 10:6, 12; cf. 6:18.

add an Abrahamic note. The land was promised to Abraham and to his seed, and in this passage the King likens the Bride to the land of promise.

In Song 4:10-15 Solomon shows the King describing the delights of the Garden the Bride will invite him to enjoy in 4:16. The King begins with an exclamation of the beauty of the Bride's love in the first line of 4:10, and the rest of 4:10-15 exposits that exclamation. The exclamation is, 'How beautiful is your love, my sister, my bride!' As with 4:9, the King is carried away with the delight he feels in response to his Bride. His transport is communicated in the words that follow, words that make clear the significance of the exclamation. Once again, these statements seem intended to communicate the biblical and theological depth of the Bride's significance to the King.

He says to her in Song 4:10, 'How much better is your love than wine, and the fragrance of your oils than any spice!' Wine comes from grapes, and oil comes from olive trees. So again, imagery is used that points to a land where the rains are regular and the soil rich. This statement also recalls what the Bride said of the King back in 1:2-3, where she said his love was better than wine and his oils fragrant. It is as though their praise for one another is echoing back and forth between them.

The King continues in Song 4:11: 'Your lips drip nectar, my bride; honey and milk are under your tongue; the fragrance of your garments is like the fragrance of Lebanon.' This statement powerfully communicates the King's delight in the Bride's kisses. Solomon's father David had said that the Bible's teachings are 'sweeter also than honey and drippings of the honeycomb' (Ps. 19:10, MT 19:11), and Solomon uses the same language in the first part of verse 11, which the ESV renders 'drip nectar.' The next statement about 'honey and milk' uses the same terminology applied to the land, 'flowing with milk and honey,' in passages like Exodus 3:8. He has summoned her from Lebanon in 4:8, and her garments must smell like the cedars of Lebanon, an aroma Solomon would have known from the construction of the temple.

Song of Songs 4:10-11 present the King telling the Bride that her love is an intoxicating power that comes with no hangover when he says it is better than wine. She is like wine, rich and strong and precious, full of pleasing aroma and robust to the palate. That her lips drip nectar and honey, and for milk to be under her tongue, likely means not just that her speech is refreshing, sweet, and nourishing but also that the experience of tasting her mouth is to him like nectar—fruit juice, honey—delicious, and milk—life-giving.

Solomon has presented the King likening the Bride to land and temple, and in Song 4:12-15 he likens her to the Garden of Eden. The terms 'garden' and 'fountain' occur in verses 12 and 15, forming a bracket around the whole of this description. She is like the garden the Lord planted in the east, and a river runs through it (cf. Gen. 2:8-10). She anticipates the eschatological temple, whence the healing stream shall flow (Ezek. 47:1-12; Zech. 13:1; Rev. 22:1-2). Solomon's description of the King here anticipates the one who will meet a Samaritan woman at a well and speak of living water (John 4:10-15).[4] Solomon poetically depicts the consummation of this marriage as an anticipation of restoration to life in the Garden of Eden.

If you will join him in esteeming marriage this way, you will not be able to despise and disregard your spouse. If you will see the cosmic significance of marriage, the way that marriage is to depict Christ laying down His life for the church, anticipating the great consummation of the purposes of God, you will not be able to lust after someone else's spouse. You will not be able to speak lightly of marriage. You will not be able to sin against the Lord, if you will hide this word in your heart and live on it.

But what, you say, of the author of this book? If this is how Solomon viewed marriage, how could he live as 1 Kings 11 says he did? We do not know whether the Song of Songs was written before or after his waywardness. If before, in the Song he said true things to which he did not himself remain true. If after, the Song can be seen as a statement of his recognition of the truth and his repudiation of his own sin.

Solomon presents the King saying in Song 4:12, 'A garden locked is my sister, my bride, a spring locked, a fountain

---

4. The reference to living water in Song 4:15 informs the references to living water John presents Jesus making in John 4:4-15 and 7:38.

sealed.' What garden in the Bible is locked, with no man allowed to enter into it? It would appear that Solomon means to allude to the cherubim guarding the way to the tree of life (Gen. 3:24). The image also speaks to the Bride's chastity. The waters that flow in this garden are for her husband alone. She is like the holy of holies, which only the high priest can enter.

In the reference to the 'orchard of pomegranates' in Song 4:13, the word rendered 'orchard' is the root from which we get the word 'paradise,' so another hint at Eden can be seen in that reference to a paradise of pomegranates. The references to 'choicest fruits' in 4:13 uses the same language found in the blessing of Moses in Deuteronomy 33:13-15. In verse 15 he calls her 'a well of living water.'

Man was driven out of Eden because Adam sinned. There's one way back into Eden: God's way. We are tempted to sin in ways that amount to trying to find some way to sneak and skulk back into Eden for ourselves, some way to steal in other than entering by the gate, through the door. Jesus said He was the gate, the door, the way, the truth. Will you enter Eden by the gate? Will you trust in Jesus? That's the only way back into the garden. If you'll trust in Jesus, you'll know the significance of the garden, of marriage, of your spouse, of the spouses of others, and of the purity of singles. Marital relations will be more than beastly reproductive practices of humanoids. Marital relations will be sacred, holy anticipations of the consummation of God's purposes.

Song 4:16–5:1: Consummation

Because of the *inclusio* in Song 4:12 and 15 with the language of 'garden' and 'fountain,' the subtitles added in the ESV seem not quite right. These subtitles have the Bride beginning to speak only at the end of verse 16. The links between 4:12 and 4:15 indicate that the Bride speaks the whole of 4:16.

The references to the day breathing in 2:17 and 4:6 anticipate what the Bride says in 4:16, 'Awake, O north wind, and come, O south wind! Blow upon my garden, let its spices flow. Let my beloved come to his garden, and eat its choicest fruits.' The King has been describing the Bride in terms reminiscent of the Garden of Eden, and now she summons the winds to blow so that all the aromas of the spices in that land might be wafted through the air to maximize the delight of her beloved. This statement captures the Bride's desire for her garden to be at its best for the King, that he might enjoy it to the full, and the boldness of this invitation she addresses to him indicates that something of the Genesis 2:25 'naked and ... not ashamed' state has been regained.

He has described the garden as locked in Song 4:12, and she invites him into the garden in 4:16. There are some doors that can only be entered by invitation of those who lock them. You might try to get in without an invitation, but you'll find that you didn't manage to get into the garden, or if you find your way in, you'll find that you're unable to enjoy being there.

The garden is locked in Song 4:12. The Bride invites the King into the garden, even calling it 'his garden,' in 4:16, and the King says in 5:1, 'I came to my garden, my sister, my bride, I gathered my myrrh with my spice, I ate my honeycomb with my honey, I drank my wine with my milk.' This poetic way of describing the consummation of the marriage recalls the comparison of her to wine, honey, and milk in 4:10-11, and to spices in 4:14, and now the King has been nourished on the Bride's love. The delicacy of the poetry takes nothing away from the delights the couple enjoy, but deepens and enriches them. This way of speaking leaves behind closed doors, between the married couple alone, what should stay behind closed doors, between the married couple alone. Expressive yet restrained; suggestive but no way indecent. The glory of what is described is matched by the glory of the description, and the nature of the description adds to the glory of what is described.

I have a friend who is a gourmand, a lover of fine food. We were once traveling together and he was reading a book on the topic, and he shared a quote with me attributed to Jean Anthelme Brillat-Savarin: 'Animals feed; man eats; the intelligent man alone knows how to eat.' Something like that is at work in this passage. Any beast can reproduce, but only human beings, those made in the image of God, those being conformed to the image of Christ, can experience what is depicted in this passage.

We are not told who speaks the words of the last line of Song 5:1, 'Eat, friends, drink, and be drunk with love!'

Solomon presented the King saying that the consummation was like drinking 'wine' in 5:1, and now there is this statement of approval. This is an encouragement to indulge, yea, to be dominated by the delights of this love. I am inclined to think that the speaker of this line is the LORD Himself. Does your concept of God include Him approving of those who gratify themselves in the delights of His gift to the point of being 'drunk with love'?

God does not put boundaries on marital relations to limit enjoyment but to maximize it.

Conclusion

Do you want to be loved this way? Maybe you've been married but it's fallen apart. Maybe you're divorced or single or widowed or for some other reason neither married nor to be married. Maybe you're struggling with homosexuality and don't think you could ever marry someone of the opposite sex. Marriage was not meant to be an idol. For that reason, I can say with confidence that even if you never marry, even if you never experience this kind of love in marriage, you can still be loved this way if you trust in Christ. What Solomon depicts in Song of Songs 4 will be fulfilled in the consummation of the relationship between Christ and the church. Trust Jesus, and everything Song of Songs 4 points to will be yours when He makes all things new.

QUESTIONS FOR DISCUSSION

1. How should our thinking about and appreciation of beauty be transformed by the way that Solomon portrays the King describing the beauty of the Bride? If the comparisons are to symbols of God's covenant blessings rather than to things she actually resembles, how should this influence our conception of beauty?

2. Would it alter your thinking and behavior to think of beauty as something befitting the Garden of Eden rather than as something to be used for worldly sex appeal?

3. What virtues and values are promoted by the presentation of the consummation of marriage as the enjoyment of exclusive access to the delights of a locked garden?

4. Why would the King and the Bride be exhorted to be drunk with love (Song 5:1)?

5. How does the consummation presented in Song of Songs 4:1–5:1 affect your hope for Christ's return?

6

Praising the Rejected One
(Song of Songs 5)

It hits her particularly when I load up all the kids to take them somewhere with her staying behind. This awareness strikes my sweet wife, and suddenly she is urging me to be careful, hugging the kids tightly, looking at me with earnest eyes, and we both know what she's thinking as she tells me that everything that is most precious to her in the world is now in that van. We're both thinking of tragic tales we've heard of those who have been bereaved of children and spouse in awful accidents.

We don't want to say goodbye in a way we would regret if, God forbid, it were to be the last time.

Need
Imagine the person who matters more to you than anyone else in the world catching you at just the wrong time. You weren't ready for them to call on you. It wasn't convenient for you to respond in accordance with their desire. To respond as they want would be the opposite of what you want.

So you say no. And they leave.

How would you feel? This person matters more to you than anyone else—you would probably change your mind! You would probably want to chase them down and respond the way this person you love wanted you to respond.

What if you couldn't find that person who mattered more to you than any other? How would you feel then?

All of that person's virtues would probably wash over you. All of your emotion for that person would well up inside you. You would long for your beloved, long for another chance to respond as you now wish you would have.

Main Point
In Song of Songs 5 the King is rejected by the Bride, who then realizes her mistake and sings his praise.

Context
In Song 1 the Bride was concerned that her appearance was dark and unattractive, and the King assured her of her beauty. She then worried that she would seem as one of the veiled women, and he told her how to find him. In Song 2 she was separated from him by a wall, and his words summoned her to himself.

Then in Song 3, the King came up out of the wilderness for his wedding day like Yahweh came up from Egypt. In Song 4 he described her as though she were the land of promise and the Garden of Eden. Then the marriage was consummated in 4:16–5:1.

Now in Song 5, the relationship between the King and the Bride seems to be patterned after the relationship between Yahweh and Israel, with the Bride rejecting the King, realizing her mistake, then describing his glory and significance.

Preview

Song 5:2-6, The Rejection of the King

Song 5:7, The Discipline of the Bride

Song 5:8-16, He Embodies Kingdom, Land, and Temple

Song 5:2-6: The Rejection of the King

An author who spent a decade writing a 1,300-page commentary on the Song has written, '5:2-8 may be the most enigmatic pericope in the Song.'[1] This is a difficult passage. We can only

---

1. Mitchell, *Song of Songs*, 878.

attempt to interpret the Song in its canonical context, with a view to the way that Solomon is summarizing and interpreting Israel's history.

We have just seen the consummation of the marriage in 4:16–5:1, and now in 5:2 the Bride tells us, 'I slept, but my heart was awake.' Some suggest that part or all of 5:2-8 is a dream. The difficulty with interpreting this as a dream is what happens in the passage. The King comes knocking and the Bride refuses to let him in (5:2-4), then she changes her mind but it's too late because he's gone by the time she gets the door open (5:5-6), and so she goes out into the city where the watchmen find her and beat her (5:7). That's a strange way for the watchmen to respond to the Queen. So strange that the suggestion that she is having a bad dream, supported by the first words of 5:2, 'I slept, but my heart was awake,' becomes appealing.

Part of the difficulty, however, has arisen from the impulse to read this passage more like narrative and less like poetry. So much of the interpretation of the Song seems to assume that there is a strict correspondence between what the poetry depicts and what actually happened in the life of the historical Solomon, as though the book were a historical narrative rather than a poetic Song.

The fact that the Song of Songs is true does not require that it present historical events that actually happened in the life of Solomon. Songs and poems that do not set out to narrate historical events can nevertheless be true. Similarly, even though the King in the Song is identified as Solomon in 3:7, 9, and 11 (cf. 1:5; 8:11, 12), this identification does not require a one-to-one correspondence between the historical Solomon and the male figure in the poem. The historical Solomon is perfectly capable of presenting an idealized version of himself in a piece of poetry that has an impressionistic narrative. That idealized depiction of himself by Solomon can be a true statement of hopes and aspirations based on God's promises and a subtle acknowledgment of the ways he himself failed.

All this is to say that, in my view, we are not reading the poetry correctly if we look for a strictly historical narrative in Song 5:2-8, or even if we look for a strictly historical report of a dream. There is a dream-like quality to this section of the Song. It is similar to what we find in ballads, songs, and poems that give us partial information, tell parts of a story, and leave the rest for us to fill in with our imagination. Songs are often evocative and hint at historical details but don't give the whole picture.

So this passage, I contend, is not to be read as a historical narrative but as an evocative piece of poetry. As we walk through it, we'll note wider correspondences Solomon may be making to Israel's history through this section of the poetry.

Yahweh married Israel at Sinai. The people committed spiritual adultery with the golden calf before they ever left the mountain. That sin showed that Israel could not keep the covenant. Just as Adam was driven out of Eden, the nation later would break the covenant and be driven out of the land.

As we have seen, Solomon presents the King in terms that remind his audience of the LORD coming up out of Egypt in 3:6-11, then the Bride is spoken of as though she is the land of promise and the Garden of Eden in 4:1-15. The consummation of the relationship is described as though the King has entered the Garden of Eden to enjoy all its beauty and bounty in 4:16–5:1. Just as Israel entered the covenant and immediately turned away from the LORD, in this passage that immediately follows the consummation of the wedding, the Bride rejects the King, who will withdraw, and then the Bride will be disciplined, after which she seeks the King.

There is a broad correspondence in this passage to what Solomon knows will happen in the history of Israel. Recognizing these correspondences does not deny that Song 5 presents a poetic depiction of an interaction between the King and his Bride. There are things for us to learn from the depiction of human love in this text. At the same time, Solomon is interpreting and summarizing Israel's history and the role of the Davidic King in God's purposes with His people.

The Bride says in 5:2:

I slept, but my heart was awake.
A sound! My beloved is knocking.[2]

---

2. By way of observation, there is a correspondence here between the way that the King, who is now married to the Bride, is outside the door, knocking, and the way that Jesus stands at His bride's door, the church at Laodicea, knocking, in Revelation 3:20. For exposition of Revelation, see my *Revelation: The Spirit Speaks to the Churches.*

The King then speaks in the next line of 5:2:

> Open to me, my sister, my love, my dove, my perfect one, for
> my head is wet with dew, my locks with the drops of the night.

He uses four phrases to address the Bride here, and then he speaks of his head being wet with dew, his hair with the drops of the night. The presentation of her as already asleep and him being wet with dew points to this being a late, inconvenient hour. So the time is not ideal for her, and he is wet from outside conditions, and now he piles up all these terms of endearment as he knocks on the door and calls for her to open to him. This is the highest concentration of terms of endearment in any one verse in the Song,[3] which would seem to indicate that the King desires intimacy with his Bride.

We see her reaction, which is true to life, in 5:3:

> I had put off my garment; how could I put it on?
> I had bathed my feet; how could I soil them?

Married people will probably recognize the familiarity of this scene. The late hour, that he's wet from the night, that she's already gone to bed, none of this bothers the man. But while he is untroubled by these realities, she cites them as the reasons this is not a good time: she's asleep and he's all wet in verse 2, and she's already undressed and bathed in verse 3. She wants to stay in bed and sleep. He wants to call her by all these special names and have her open to him, and the fact that she's already taken off her garment is no problem.

The King and the Bride are clearly in different frames of mind, and they clearly desire different things. If this is your experience in marriage, you are not alone, and you are not experiencing something new. Solomon could describe this three thousand years ago.

The King is depicted in the Song acting in a way that is both loving and instructive. He hears his Bride's concerns and goes away, but not before leaving a blessing. The Bride relates in 5:4-5:

> My beloved put his hand to the latch,
> and my heart was thrilled within me.

---

3. Mitchell, *Song of Songs*, 881.

> I arose to open to my beloved, and my hands dripped with
> myrrh,
> my fingers with liquid myrrh, on the handles of the bolt.

The King's conduct in the situation seems to cause a change
of heart in the Bride. She describes him putting his hand to
the latch, and from what happens we see what he has done.
He has put myrrh on the lock. He has accepted her demurral,
her refusal, and he has left a blessing behind. This causes her
heart to churn within her, and she gets out of bed and opens
the door.

Notice how the King did not respond. He didn't wheedle.
He didn't plead. He didn't argue. He heard her concerns, and
apparently he loves her enough to put her desire to remain in
bed above his own desire for her to open to him, so he leaves
a blessing and goes away.

Let's consider the Bride's initial response: it's inconvenient
to be awakened in the middle of the night, to have to get out
of bed (perhaps it's cold), put something on, and soil washed
feet. Those are inconveniences, but are they worth the refusal
of her husband? Are these selfish concerns? From her reaction
in 5:4-5, she seems to decide that her concerns did not warrant
her refusal of the King's overtures.

What do we learn from the possibility that Solomon
meant to present the King such that he represented Yahweh,
and the Bride such that she represented Israel in the Song?
If we consider this scene from that angle, the poetry might
suggest the ways that Yahweh imposes minor inconveniences
on His people. Should they refuse Him because they will be
inconvenienced? They exist for Him. He redeemed them. He
has given them the land of promise. He protects them from
their enemies. He provides all good things for them. And they
won't be bothered by Him?

Like the King in this scene, Yahweh does not withdraw all
the benefits He has given people when they refuse Him. Often
when people refuse the Lord, He leaves behind a blessing that
prompts people to seek Him.

The Bride next relates in Song 5:6:

> I opened to my beloved, but my beloved had turned and
> gone.

My soul failed me when he spoke.
I sought him, but found him not; I called him, but he gave no
answer.

So the Bride opens the door and the King is gone. I think the
NASB has a better rendering of the phrase 'My soul failed me.'
The NASB has 'went out,' so I would render the line, 'My soul
went out when he spoke.' The idea is that she felt love for him
as he spoke to her. In that last line of verse 6 the Bride says
things that are reminiscent of statements elsewhere in the Old
Testament.

In Proverbs 1:28 Lady Wisdom warns those who will not
heed her that when the consequences of their rebellion come
upon them, 'they will call upon me, but I will not answer;
they will seek me diligently but will not find me.' Hosea 5:6
says, 'With their flocks and herds they shall go to seek the
LORD, but they will not find him; he has withdrawn from
them.' Amos 8:12 says, 'They shall run to and fro, to seek the
word of the LORD, but they shall not find it.' Solomon wrote
Proverbs, and what he said in Proverbs 1:28 and Song 5:6 may
have influenced what Hosea and Amos wrote.

Song 5:7: The Discipline of the Bride

Moses prophesied in Leviticus 26, Deuteronomy 4:25-31, and
Deuteronomy 28–32 that Israel would break the covenant,
be disciplined and exiled from the land, then experience
restoration and the fulfillment of God's promises. When
Solomon prayed at the dedication of the temple in 1 Kings 8,
his words on that occasion show that he understood what
Moses said (see 1 Kings 8:22-53).

Just as Moses and Solomon envisioned Israel coming under
discipline for rejecting the LORD, the Bride is disciplined in
Song 5:7:

The watchmen found me as they went about in the city;
they beat me, they bruised me, they took away my veil,
those watchmen of the walls.

At the human level, these watchmen are patrolling the city,
and we have already encountered them in Song 3:3, as there

too the Bride was seeking the King. Here the watchmen punish the Bride, physically beating her.

There are other texts in the Bible where 'watchmen' are prophetic figures whom the Lord uses to watch over, and in some cases proclaim judgment against, His people. In some places, the same term that we find here in the Song is used to describe the watchmen (Isa. 62:6; cf. Jer. 51:12). Other texts use synonymous terms for the watchmen (Isa. 56:10; Jer. 6:17; 31:6; Ezek. 3:17; 33:2, 6, 7; Hosea 9:8 Micah 7:4). The parallels between the King and the Bride and Yahweh and Israel might inform the references to the watchmen in the Song. Just as the watchmen helped the Bride find the King in Song 3:3, the prophets—chiefly Moses—mediated Israel's relationship with Yahweh. Just as the watchmen visited justice on the Bride for refusing the King in Song 5:7, the prophets announced judgment on Israel for rejecting Yahweh.

Song 5:8-16: He Embodies Kingdom, Land, and Temple

The Bride's adjuration of the daughters of Jerusalem in 5:8 prompts them to ask her why her beloved is so special in 5:9, and she tells them about him in 5:10-16. In this passage Solomon presents the Bride describing the King as one who embodies the Kingdom, the Land, and the Temple.

The Bride's adjuration in 5:8 starts out like earlier adjurations in 2:7 and 3:5 (cf. 8:4), but this time she wants the daughters of Jerusalem to tell the King that she is sick with love. This lovesickness seems to result from the King's withdrawal in 5:6 and the discipline the Bride suffered in 5:7. The daughters of Jerusalem ask her why she adjures them thus in 5:9, offering the Bride the opportunity to extol the glories of the King.

The King's description of the Bride in Song 4 was not about her physical appearance but about her spiritual and theological significance to the King. The King described her as the land of promise and the Garden of Eden, probably because these blessings speak of what matters most to him, the Kingdom of God. The Bride will now describe the King in the same way. She speaks of how he embodies the Davidic Kingdom, of how he is like the land of promise blessed by God, and of how he is like the temple dwelling in the midst of the land. These descriptions show us what matters most to the

King and the Bride: God and His purposes. These descriptions also point to the deeper reality that the marriage between the King and his Bride represents. The King represents Yahweh, the Bride represents God's people, and their union symbolizes the enjoyment of the covenant between God and His people in the land. Israel's relationship with Yahweh gives them life.

As the Bride answers the question from daughters of Jerusalem about what makes her beloved so special, she begins by speaking of the King in terms that remind us of David, who was described as 'ruddy' in 1 Samuel 16:12 and 17:42. She says in Song 5:10: 'My beloved is radiant and ruddy, distinguished among ten thousand.'

In the midst of a myriad of men, the Bride declares, her beloved would stand out. That he is physically attractive to her is doubtless true, but what she says here goes beyond beauty to significance. Her beloved is the Davidic King. The reference to 'ten thousand' is reminiscent of the song that Saul had slain his thousands, David his tens of thousands (1 Sam. 18:7; 21:11; 29:5).

There are several features of Song of Songs 5:10-16 that seem to have provided the terms and concepts later employed by Daniel as he described the statue in Nebuchadnezzar's dream detailed in Daniel 2. If this is correct, Daniel would have been thoroughly familiar with the Song of Songs, and then when Nebuchadnezzar's dream was revealed to him, the terms he found ready to hand for describing that statue came from his awareness of this passage in Song 5. The Bride describes the radiance of the King in Song 5:10. Daniel described the statue in Nebuchadnezzar's dream as shimmering with 'exceeding brightness' (Dan. 2:31). Song 5 is in Hebrew whereas Daniel 2:31 is in Aramaic, so the same terms are not used. The concepts and symbolism, however, are synonymous. The statue was of Nebuchadnezzar and the kingdoms that followed him (2:38-40). Here in Song 5 the Bride will describe the King, and just as Daniel does with the statue, she speaks of his head, his arms, his body, legs, and bases (feet) (Song 5:11, 14, 15; cf. Dan. 2:32-33, 38-43).

Since Solomon lived and wrote in the 900s B.C., with Daniel living later in the 500s B.C., in view of the fact that

Scriptural writings were likely memorized in ancient Israel,[4] it seems that what Solomon wrote influenced Daniel. Daniel being aware of and shaped by texts like Song 5, when he beheld in vision (Dan. 2:19) the content of Nebuchadnezzar's dream, his perception of that dream and its meaning were informed by what he knew from biblical texts like Song 5. The evidence indicates that Daniel's presentation of the contents of Nebuchadnezzar's dream was shaped in vocabulary and structure by Song 5.

What would the influence of the language and structure of Song 5:10-16 on Daniel show us about the meaning of this passage in the Song of Songs? If Daniel uses the language and imagery in a passage that has the king embodying the kingdom, it would confirm the idea that the imagery functions the same way in the Song of Songs. The vision in Daniel 2 clearly pertains to the king, Nebuchadnezzar, to his kingdom and those that would follow him. With the two passages using similar concepts, structure, and imagery, it is likely that the two depictions symbolize similar realities.

By putting these descriptions on the lips of the Bride in the Song, Solomon depicts the King of Israel as an embodiment of God's kingdom. Like the image Daniel saw, with the head of 'fine gold' (Dan. 2:32), the Bride describes the King saying in Song 5:11, 'His head is finest gold.' The next lines of Song 5:11 show that this is not to be taken literally, as she goes on to say that 'his locks are wavy, black as a raven.' Since ravens are unclean animals, this description is probably pointing to the color of the King's hair. Since 'ruddy' points to redness, and gold is yellowish, if 'black as a raven' points to real color, the gold and ruddy hues are likely figurative descriptions, probably pointing to the quality and wisdom of the King and his place in the Davidic line.

Song 5:12 and 5:13 bring in images that point to the way that the King represents the blessed land of promise, before 5:14 returns to descriptions that correspond to Daniel 2. The King said to the Bride in Song 1:15 and 4:1, 'your eyes are doves,' and now she says of him:

---

4. See the chapter, 'The Psalms as an Anthology to be Memorized,' in Gordon J. Wenham, *Psalms as Torah: Reading Biblical Song Ethically* (Grand Rapids: Baker, 2012), 41-56.

His eyes are like doves beside streams of water,
bathed in milk, sitting beside a full pool.

Some suggest that this description points to the way his eyes actually look, but as with the use of this imagery in Song 4, I think in 5:12 it points to animal life in the land, with verse 13 speaking of the spices and flowers that grow in it:

His cheeks are like beds of spices, mounds of sweet-smelling herbs.
His lips are lilies, dripping liquid myrrh.

Just as the King's description of the Bride in Song 4 spoke of her eyes, hair, teeth, lips, cheeks, neck, and chest, moving downward, so the Bride's description of the King started with his head, moved to hair, eyes, cheeks, lips, and in 5:14 moves down to his arms:

His arms are rods of gold, set with jewels.
His body is polished ivory, bedecked with sapphires.

Whereas the statue in Daniel 2 symbolizes different kingdoms, the Kingdom Solomon represents is the one that will last forever (cf. 2 Sam. 7:13; Dan. 2:44). So as we move down this statue it's all one Kingdom. There are different Hebrew words used for gold in this context, and alabaster will come in, too, but these changes in material do not point to different kingdoms as the changes in material do in Daniel 2. The materials in Song 5 all point, in various ways, to the Davidic Kingdom and the temple.

The word rendered 'jewels' in Song 5:14 could be transliterated 'tarshish,' and Christopher Mitchell writes,

Tarshish (along with sapphire) is part of the biblical depiction of mankind's original holy state in the presence of God in Eden; God's redemption of fallen mankind; and the eschatological state of the redeemed, in which God's people will once again possess perfect holiness and righteousness in the presence of God.[5]

---

5. Mitchell, *Song of Songs*, 930, citing Ezekiel 28:13-14; Genesis 2:11-12; Revelation 21:19-21; 22:1-5.

As for the 'ivory' in the description of his body, this is reminiscent of Solomon's throne, built of ivory in 1 Kings 10:18, along with the 'ivory palaces' mentioned in Psalm 45:8. Psalm 21:3 speaks of a 'crown of fine gold,' perhaps alluded to when the Bride says his head is 'finest gold' in Song 5:11. The jewels and sapphires mentioned in 5:14 are also reminiscent of the jewels in the breastpiece of the high priest (Exod. 28:15-23).

In Song 5:15 the Bride says of the King:

> His legs are alabaster columns, set on bases of gold.
> His appearance is like Lebanon, choice as the cedars.

The word rendered 'alabaster' here is related to the word rendered 'marble' in the description of what David provided for the building of the temple in 1 Chronicles 29:2. The word rendered 'bases' is used repeatedly for various joins in the instructions for the tabernacle, and as everything in tabernacle and temple was overlaid with gold, so it is here. Then the reference to the cedars of Lebanon calls to mind the wood Solomon got from Hiram for the building of the temple (1 Kings 5:1-12). The Bride says the King looks like cedars of Lebanon, as though his appearance puts her in mind of the temple.[6]

This depiction, then, captures the way that the idealized King Solomon of the Song's poetry embodies the Kingdom, the way that his just rule ensures the blessing of God on the land of promise and the presence of God in the temple he built. As the King did for the Bride, the Bride has extolled the King in terms of his spiritual and theological significance for the purposes of God in the Kingdom of David.

In Song 5:16 the Bride says something that reflects what the King has done for the Bride in the Song, and what the Word of God has done for God's people:

> His mouth is most sweet, and he is altogether desirable.
> This is my beloved and this is my friend, O daughters of
>   Jerusalem.

Commentators often remark that this points to the Bride enjoying the King's kisses. Indeed. But his words, words

---

6. A King will come to Israel who will speak of Himself as the temple to be torn down and resurrected (John 2:19-22).

which overcame her insecurity about her appearance and standing in Song 1, words which overcame the separation between them twain in Song 2, are probably also in view. The King speaks sweetly to her, as God does to His people (cf. Hosea 2:14). David said of God's words in Psalm 19:10 that they are 'More to be desired ... than gold, even much fine gold; sweeter also than honey and drippings of the honeycomb.'

Conclusion

The King in Song 5 represents Yahweh, who entered into a covenant with His Bride—Israel—at Sinai, only to be rejected by and withdraw from her. Like the Bride in Song 5, Israel was disciplined as the watchmen—the prophets—announced Yahweh's judgment against her. The purpose of Yahweh's discipline was to make Israel realize how good Yahweh is, to make them jealous for His love (cf. Deut. 32:21).

The story doesn't end in Song 5, for Israel or the Bride. In Song 5:10-16 the Bride sings the praises of the King she rejected. This poetic depiction will find its culmination and fulfillment in the one who embodies in Himself Kingdom, Land, and Temple. The pattern of the rejected bridegroom is fulfilled in the rejected one whose praises we sing. The pattern of the rejected one whose people sing His praise finds its ultimate expression in the Lord Jesus.

> Jesus stands at the door and knocks.
> Jesus speaks sweet words to His beloved.
> Jesus summons us to inconvenience ourselves that we might experience His love.
> Jesus calls us to leave our comforts that we might know Him.

How will you answer His call? Will you cause Him to withdraw from you, even if He leaves a blessing behind? Or will you fling the door wide for Him to fill your life? There is nothing better than Jesus!

> Jesus will reign in the Kingdom that can never be shaken.
> Jesus will cause the desert to bloom.
> Jesus is the high priest of Israel, and He is the temple of the new creation.
> Jesus is our beloved.
> Jesus is our friend.

QUESTIONS FOR DISCUSSION

1. Is it difficult for you to conceive of a poem or work of art telling the truth even when not presenting a strictly historical narrative?

2. If this is not a strictly historical narrative, or a narrative of a historical dream, does that alter the way Song of Songs 5 is to be understood?

3. At the level of the human King and Bride, what happens in this chapter?

4. Does what happens between the human King and Bride in the chapter correspond to the history of Yahweh's relationship with Israel?

5. How would you interpret the symbolism and imagery the Bride uses to describe the King in Song of Songs 5:10-16?

7

Are the Vines in Bloom?
(Song of Songs 6)

Have you ever blown it? Blown it and thought that maybe there was no making things right? Maybe you've had experiences like I've had. There have been times when I thought I had done damage that was too severe to be set right. Things that I've done that I thought were going to cost me a relationship, cost me a friendship, cost me respect I could never regain.

Have you ever done something so bad that you thought your mistake was going to be the last word on the matter?

If you're a Christian, I suspect you've also seen, as I have, the truth of Proverbs 28:13: 'Whoever conceals his transgressions will not prosper, but he who confesses and forsakes them will obtain mercy.' If you're a Christian and you've blown it, my guess is that in these instances you've confessed your sin, forsaken it, and experienced God's mercy.

If you've blown it, repented, confessed, and experienced mercy, you might have noticed something else, too. In a mysterious way, God is able to show you deeper aspects of His love as you experience His forgiveness. He is able to make you feel afresh the good news of the cross when it feels like the backs of your eyeballs are scratchy because of your sin.

God's grace rests heaviest on those who feel themselves lowest.

Need

We need a Savior stronger than our sin, don't we?

We need a covenant partner whose commitment is stronger than our waywardness.

We need a lover whose devotion will not be destroyed by our ignorance and weakness.

We need that grace greater than all our sin,

that cross that conquers the curse,

that life that death cannot undo,

that hope that will not disappoint,

that love that will not let us go.

We need our Bridegroom.

We need Jesus, and we need Him to love us the way the King loves the Bride in Song of Songs 6.

Main Point

In Song of Songs 6 the King's love for the Bride causes her to repent of refusing him, convinces her to seek him, and has him prepared to sweep her up as soon as she returns to him.

Preview

Song 6:1-3, The Daughters and the Bride

Song 6:4-10, What He Said to Her

Song 6:11-13, Are the Vines in Bloom?

Song 6:1-3: The Daughters and the Bride

The question in Song of Songs 6:1 is reminiscent of the question in 5:9 *both* in the words spoken *and* in the syntactical structure of the phrases. In the impressionistic drama that the Song is presenting, in 5:3 the Bride rejected the King, then changed her mind and sought him but could not find him (5:6). She adjured the daughters of Jerusalem to communicate her lovesickness (5:8), in response to which they asked their first question in 5:9. Her answer to their first question elaborated on the King's distinctive appeal in 5:10-16, and she closed that statement with a reference to the daughters of Jerusalem at the end of 5:16.

This context indicates that the daughters of Jerusalem ask a second question in 6:1. They asked what set the King apart in 5:9, and they ask where he has gone in 6:1. In her adjuration in 5:8, she called on them to communicate her lovesickness to him if they found him. Now in 6:1 they ask where he has gone that they might seek him and do what she has adjured them to do.

What the Bride says in Song 6:2 is enigmatic for several reasons. On the one hand, there is no indication prior to her words in 6:2 that she has found the King or that someone has told her where he is. On the other hand, where she says he has gone is very much open to interpretation. She says:

> My beloved has gone down to his garden to the beds of spices,
> to graze in the gardens and to gather lilies.

So we have at least two questions to answer. First, how does Solomon intend us to understand how the Bride now knows where the King has gone? Second, and this flows out of the first, what does she mean when she says he 'has gone down to his garden'? In 4:12 he calls her a garden. Then in 4:16 she says, 'Let my beloved come to his garden,' followed by 5:1, where he says, 'I came to my garden.' So *she* could be the garden. If she is the garden, however, how does that fit in context? Is she reflecting on him coming to her in 5:2, in response to which she turned him away in 5:3, then could not find him in 5:6? We could understand 6:2 to indicate that he has 'gone down to his garden' in the sense that he has returned to her. If that is the case, it would follow naturally that the King speaks to her face-to-face again in 6:4-10.

Another possibility, though, is that the garden in 6:2 is not a figurative reference to the Bride but a real place, a garden (cf. 'the king's garden' in Jeremiah 39:4), that the King visits when he leaves the Bride (5:6). This seems to fit better with the context: the Bride refused the King in 5:3, sought but could not find him in 5:6, adjured the daughters of Jerusalem to give him a message in 5:8, and now in 6:2, from her knowledge of him, she states where she thinks he is. If this is the case, the King's words in 6:4-10 are not the King speaking directly to her but her thinking on something he has already said. I think this is likely because in 6:11 she decides to go to the 'garden' (rendered 'orchard' in the ESV) to find her beloved.

Whichever way we take this, we again have a pattern of the King's words and actions bringing about reconciliation. Whether the Bride and King are reunited by his return to her, his figurative garden, in 6:2, or whether the King has gone to a literal garden in 6:2 and then she reflected on things he said to her in 6:4-10, prompting her to go to the garden to look for him in 6:11, either way the Bride repents of her behavior toward the blameless King, whose character prompted her to seek him.

Solomon's depiction of the King's behavior in the poetry is instructive for husbands and wives, but it is particularly relevant to the way that husbands respond to their wives. The King communicated desires the Bride did not share in 5:2, and when she refused him in 5:3, his response was loving and honorable. He left the blessing of myrrh on the lock and withdrew. It seems from 6:2 that the Bride has realized that the King has gone to his garden refuge. This garden is characterized by luxurious 'beds of spices' (6:2; cf. 5:13), and she compares the King to a gazelle who 'grazes.' The King does not graze in a rough pasture among weeds but among lilies. This picture of grazing in lilies suggests the King's prosperity, wealth, and cultivation of the ground to the point that he need not graze among weeds that grow at random in open fields but can do so in gardens among lilies.

Solomon portrays the Bride reflecting on the King in his garden in 6:2, prompting her to make a statement that reverses her refusal in 5:3, when she says in 6:3,

> I am my beloved's and my beloved is mine;
> he grazes among the lilies.

Similar statements can be found in 2:16 and 7:10, but this one stands out for its repudiation of her earlier reluctance to open to him. She now declares herself to be his.

Solomon's Song is true to life. This is no airbrushed, photoshopped, emo-music in the background, sentimental, movie-fake-relationship out of Hollywood. This poem depicts the reality of the human condition, where real people with real frustrations *really can* conduct themselves such that love prevails. Don't give up. The path to this kind of love is the path Jesus walked. The way to be this kind of spouse is to pursue Christ-likeness.

If you're an unbeliever, the first thing you need to do is take a long look at what Jesus did. Perfect God, He humbled Himself to take on human flesh, enter this world, and die on the cross to pay the penalty for sin. He did that to make a way for people to be made right with God and to show what love looks like, what love does. If you will turn from your sin and trust in Christ, the Spirit of God will enable you to live similar to how Jesus did, laying down your life for others as He did.

Believers are called to follow in the footsteps of Jesus (1 Pet. 2:21), husbands loving their wives as Christ loved the church (Eph. 5:25).

Song 6:4-10: What He Said to Her

In Song 6:4-10 Solomon portrays the Bride reflecting on the King's words. Solomon does not present the King speaking 6:4-10 in the Bride's presence, because the Bride goes to the garden to seek him in 6:11, the King sweeping her up in his love in 6:12.

She realizes where he has gone in 6:2, reflects on what he has said to her in 6:4-10, then goes to find him in 6:11.

Song 6:4 and 6:10 both end with the words 'awesome as an army with banners.' That phrase brackets this section. Solomon presents the Bride ruminating on words the King had said to her at some point previously, beginning in 6:4:

> You are beautiful as Tirzah, my love,
> lovely as Jerusalem,
> awesome as an army with banners.

The Hebrew word *tirzah* (תרצה) means 'beautiful,' and the city of Tirzah was probably so named because it was a beautiful place. In 1 Kings 14–15 we see that the city of Tirzah was an early capital of the northern kingdom of Israel after it separated from Judah. In Solomon's day the kingdom was united and Tirzah would have been a significant northern city. So Solomon picks this significant city in the north to conjoin with Jerusalem as he portrays the King articulating his admiration for his beloved: she is like the great cities north and south in the land. Again his admiration for her beauty is expressed in terms of the land of promise and the kingdom of God.

Given the way that Solomon has presented the King describing the Bride's beauty in kingdom terms, we can see why he would liken her to an awe-inspiring army with banners. He speaks of his love for her in terms of the land teeming with life, lush like the Garden of Eden, so why would he not liken her to the hosts of the army of Israel, which fights the LORD's battles?

Apart from the first phrase of 6:5, the body of 6:5-7 restates what the King said to the Bride in 4:1-3. In that context, the King had entered Jerusalem for the wedding in 3:6-11, spoken to the Bride in 4:1-15, then consummated the marriage in 4:16–5:1. Given the repetition of 4:1-3 in 6:5-7, it appears that in 6:8-10 the Bride continues to reflect on things the King said to her.

In the first phrase of Song 6:5 the King communicates his inability to withstand the Bride's gaze. Her eyes are too much for him, overwhelming him. Having said that, 6:5b-7 restates 4:1-3 with only slight alterations. This repetition fits the suggestion that the Bride and the King are not yet reunited but the Bride now reflects on the King's earlier statements to her.

The interpretation of Song of Songs 6:8-9 cannot be extricated from conclusions about the wider context. That is, my view that Solomon is presenting an idealized version of himself rather than his own personal history informs my understanding of 6:8-9. In these verses Solomon portrays the Bride reflecting on the way the King said to her:

> There are sixty queens and eighty concubines,
> and virgins without number.
> My dove, my perfect one, is the only one,
> the only one of her mother,
> pure to her who bore her.
> The young women saw her and called her blessed;
> the queens and concubines also, and they praised her.

This study takes the Song of Solomon to be *poetry* found in the *Bible*. In this poetry, the author, Solomon, does not depict his own life story (replete with his own sordid history) but presents an idealized character who bears his name. Solomon does this because he is not writing an autobiographical, historical narrative. Rather, he is writing a poem that interprets and summarizes the big story of the Bible. In that big story, a seed of the woman was promised, and as the story unfolds it becomes clear that the seed of the woman will be the King from the line of David who will bring to pass the blessing of Abraham (cf. Ps. 72). We should not, therefore, allow our knowledge of the historical Solomon to control our understanding of Song of Songs 6:8-9.

There are many ways in which our knowledge of the historical Solomon, particularly what we find in 1 Kings 11, could taint our interpretation of the Song of Songs. If we attempt to read the poetry as history, in view of what 1 Kings 11 tells us about Solomon's wives and concubines, we might suppose Solomon distinguishes the Bride from the rest of the women in his harem in Song 6:8-9. Would a woman in any culture in any place or time find comfort in the fact that her husband told her that of all the many women he enjoys she is his favorite? In view of the fact that the Song of Songs has been recognized as inspired by the Holy Spirit, and in view of God's monogamous intention for human sexuality (Matt. 19:4-5), I find it unlikely that these verses present the King telling the Bride that she is his favorite among all his women.

That, however, is not the only way to understand Song of Songs 6:8-9. The verse does not say that the queens, concubines, and virgins constitute Solomon's harem. The verse simply says these women exist.[1] If we read the poetry not as a historical account but as Solomon's poetic depiction of an idealized version of himself, these statements can be seen as distinguishing the Bride from other queens who are married to other kings, from concubines other men have, and from other young women of marriageable age.

The Bride can thus be understood to reflect on the King communicating something along these lines to her: *we have*

---

1. Rightly Estes in Fredericks and Estes, *Ecclesiastes and the Song of Songs*, 384: 'it also should be noted that Solomon here states only that these women exist; he does not explicitly say that they belong to him (cf. the similar numerical language in Prov. 30:15, 18, 21, 29).'

interacted with sixty other kings whose queens you have met, and in our interactions with different people you know of eighty concubines, and you are well aware that there are many unmarried virgins in the land: as far as I am concerned you are the only woman in the world. If this understanding of Song 6:8-9 is correct, Solomon understood his own conduct, narrated in 1 Kings 11, to be sinful and repudiated it.

This way of understanding these verses also makes sense of the stress on the uniqueness of the Bride in Song 6:9:

> My dove, my perfect one, is the only one,
> the only one of her mother,
> pure to her who bore her.
> The young women saw her and called her blessed;
> the queens and concubines also, and they praised her.

We need not read the first line of 6:9 as the King hypocritically, even cynically, speaking of this unique woman who is the 'only one' when he has a harem full of women. Nor need we see the second line as him commenting on how the rest of the harem saw that he had a favorite.

Rather, if the King in the Song is a stylized Solomon rather than the historical Solomon, we can allow the poetry to depict for us the monogamous union the historical Solomon did not enjoy. The 'young women' in 6:9 might be identified with the 'daughters of Jerusalem' referenced elsewhere in the Song, the 'queens' being the wives of the kings of other lands, and the 'concubines' being women not treated as well as the Bride is by the King.

Read as I am suggesting we read it, the poetry presents the Bride reflecting on how the King assured her that she was unique to him in Song 6:8, and other women saw her unique position and acknowledged the glory of it in 6:9.

This section opened in 6:4 with a statement about the Bride's beauty being like two great cities in Israel, and it closes in 6:10 with a statement about the Bride's beauty being like the two great lights of creation:

> Who is this who looks down like the dawn,
> beautiful as the moon, bright as the sun,
> awesome as an army with banners?

The description of the Bride's beauty in terms of two cities of Israel, north and south, has obvious connections to land and kingdom (does this have anything to do with husband and wife?). This comparison of her beauty to the dawn, to the moon, and to the sun depicts her as embodying the features of Joseph's dream, where the sun (father) and moon (mother) and eleven stars (brothers) bowed to Joseph (Gen. 37:9-10). The same imagery is at work in Revelation 12:1, where the woman who represents Israel and Mary is clothed with the sun, with the moon under her feet, and wears a crown of twelve stars. Once again she is as breathtaking as an army in martial array (6:10; cf. 6:4). These comparisons of the Bride's beauty liken her to God's land and God's people, just as the King is identified with Yahweh and His Messiah.

Song 6:11-13: Are the Vines in Bloom?
In Song 6:11 the Bride says:

> I went down to the nut orchard
> to look at the blossoms of the valley,
> to see whether the vines had budded,
> whether the pomegranates were in bloom.

We could render the phrase 'nut orchard' as 'garden of nuts,' because the word rendered 'orchard' is the same term rendered 'garden' in 6:2. The reuse of this word indicates that in 6:2 Solomon depicts the Bride realizing where the King has gone, in response to which she reflected on his assuring words to her (6:4-10), and now in 6:11 she sets out to seek him where she knows him to be.

The remainder of Song 6:11 indicates that she is not quite sure what she will find when she gets there. After the King invited her to come away with him in Song 2:10-14, we read in 2:15, 'our vineyards are in blossom.' As the King extols the Bride in 4:13-15, the fruit is clearly in season, with the King relishing the choicest fruits of the garden in 4:16–5:1.

Now, however, after the Bride's refusal of the King in 5:3, as she sets out to find him in his garden (6:2), she indicates in 6:11 that she does not know 'whether the vines had budded, whether the pomegranates were in bloom.' These statements point not merely to the season of the year but also to the season of their relationship. The Bride goes to find the King, and she is not certain whether she will find that their love is ripe or whether she will find that more time is needed before they can again enjoy the sweet fruit of their love.

Song 6:12 is notoriously difficult,[2] but if the conclusions reached here about the context and the suggestiveness of the poetry are correct, we see that in 6:12 things go better for the Bride than she had anticipated. The ESV renders 6:12 thus,

> Before I was aware, my desire set me
> among the chariots of my kinsman, a prince.

Read in context, the Bride has gone down to the garden where she thinks the King will be. She goes to see 'whether the vines had budded' (Song 6:11). She goes to see how they stand with one another, how the King will receive her after she rejected him in 5:3. To her delighted surprise, the King sweeps her up in his chariots.

So in this unfolding impressionistic drama, in Song 6:12 Solomon portrays the King having made preparation for the Bride's attempt to seek him. When she comes, as he expected her to do, he welcomes her back with enthusiasm. The vines have budded. The pomegranates are in bloom (cf. Song 6:11).

Song 6:13 brings in the cheers of those who accompany the King. They are now celebrating the Bride's return to him:

> Return, return, O Shulammite,
> return, return, that we may look upon you.

The King's companions celebrate her return, and they want to see the glory of the King reflected in the beauty of the Bride. In response to this, the King joins in the celebration with what seems to be a rhetorical question intended to augment the glory of the Bride's beauty at the end of Song 6:13:

> Why should you look upon the Shulammite,
> as upon a dance before two armies?

---

2. Thus G. Lloyd Carr, *The Song of Solomon: An Introduction and Commentary* (Downers Grove: InterVarsity, 1984), 151-2 can write, 'Commentators are unanimous that this verse is the most difficult in the Song and one of the most difficult in the Old Testament to make sense of.'

The reason for looking at her has been repeatedly stated throughout the Song. She has thrice been called the 'most beautiful among women' (Song 1:8; 5:9; 6:1). It would be natural for the King's subjects to want to see the Bride's beauty, particularly as she is reunited with the King.

In Song 6:13 the Bride is twice referred to as the Shulammite. This is the only place in the Song where she is so named. The term has been understood as the feminine form of Solomon's own name. The similarity between the names *Solomon* and *Shulammite* suggests that Solomon has chosen to refer to her this way to provoke reflection on this aspect of the poetry. There is another instance in the Bible of a woman receiving a name derived from that of the man, the Hebrew term for man, *ish*, being the basis for the Hebrew term for woman, *ishah* (Gen. 2:23). In the poetry of the Song, Solomon portrays the King's words giving confidence, standing, and access to the Bride. As the relationship develops, he invited her to come away with him in chapter 2, arrived for the wedding day in chapter 3, then celebrated the marriage in 4:1–5:1. When the King married the Bride, his status became her status. He was the King, and she became his Queen when the covenant between them was made. The Shulammite derives her identity from Solomon.

As a biblical theologian thoroughly acquainted with the Scripture available to him, Solomon would no doubt have been aware of the way that when Yahweh entered into covenant with Israel, a new status was conveyed upon the nation. Indeed, the very name of *Israel* derived from the patriarch's interaction with Yahweh (Gen. 32:28). The character of Yahweh sanctified Israel. The covenant between Yahweh and Israel is dramatized as a marriage, hinted at in the Song of Songs, anticipating the fulfillment of the meaning of marriage in the covenant between Christ and His Bride.

Conclusion
What else might Solomon intend to communicate about the relationship between Yahweh and Israel in Song 6?

Consider the broad-angle parallels between what we see in the poetry of the Song and what Solomon would have known about the past and future of Israel's history:

- Israel came out of Egypt, entered into a marital-covenant with Yahweh, who led them through the wilderness, His tabernacle in their midst, the ark His footstool.

- In Song 3:6-11 the King, Yahweh's image and likeness, comes out of the wilderness to enter Jerusalem for 'the day of his wedding,' then the King describes his Bride as though she is the land of promise and the Garden of Eden.

- Moses predicted that Israel would enter the land, break the covenant, be exiled from the land, then restored to fellowship with Yahweh. Hosea spoke of the restoration as a new marriage. Jeremiah called it a new covenant. Solomon prayed for these very things at the dedication of the temple (1 Kings 8).

- No sooner has the King wed the Bride in the Song than she refuses him (Song 5:3), just as Israel rejected Yahweh.

- Just as Israel sought Yahweh and could not find him, so the Bride sought the King and could not find him (Song 5:6).

- Just as the prophets announced judgment against Israel, the watchmen punished the Bride (5:7).

- Just as Israel sought Yahweh in exile, Daniel and Nehemiah confessing sin and praying for restoration, so the Bride adjured the daughters of Jerusalem to communicate her longing for the King (5:8).

- When Israel's prophets pointed forward to the restoration, they spoke of it as a return to the land, and the return to the land was described as a return to the garden of Eden. When the Bride in the Song has repented of her rejection of the King and seeks him, she realizes that he is in his garden (Song 6:2). She then recalls the King's loving words to her, before going to the garden to seek him (6:11).

- On the way she was swept up in his chariots (6:12), and soon the poetry will communicate a reversal of the curses (7:10) before showing another 'coming up from the wilderness' in 8:5. It is as though Solomon depicts their reunion as a new exodus and return from exile.

The Song of Songs is a poem in the Bible. The poetry of the Song depicts human love, and we have much to learn from what Solomon shows with his words. The poetry summarizes and interprets the big story of the Bible, and the love between the King and the Bride points beyond itself to the fulfillment of marriage in the consummation of the relationship between Christ and the church. Marriage was not made for us to make an idol of it. Marriage was made to help us anticipate its fulfillment when the Bridegroom returns for the Bride He made spotless by His blood.

Questions for Discussion

1. What does it say about their relationship that after the King has withdrawn (Song 5:6), the Bride nevertheless knows where he is (6:2)?

2. Do you agree with the interpretation of Song of Songs 6:8-9 offered in this chapter? If not, how do you understand those verses?

3. Solomon is a man of peace (his name is related to *shalom*), and yet in this chapter he mentions armies three times—6:4, 10, and 13. Why do you think the Bride is compared to an army?

4. In times of conflict, do you reflect on the loving things your spouse has said, as the Bride does in Song of Songs 6:4-10, or do your thoughts dwell on ways you can indict your spouse?

5. The King welcomes the Bride back with enthusiasm in Song of Songs 6:11-13. When your spouse comes to apologize to you, is your response receptive and enthusiastic or reluctant and resistant?

8

Reconciliation
(Song of Songs 7)

The Song opens with the Bride celebrating the King (Song 1:2-4), then articulating her anxiety about her own appearance (1:5-6) and about her standing in the community (1:7). The King spoke words to her that assured her of her beauty and granted her access to himself (1:8-11). The couple then exulted together in their love (1:12–2:7). The Bride next related how a wall separated her from the King (2:8-9), in response to which the King invited her to join him in marriage (2:10-17). The Bride recounted how she longed for the King in anticipation of the wedding, noting how she encountered the watchmen as she sought him (3:1-5). The King then entered Jerusalem for the wedding like Yahweh Himself in solemn procession up from the wilderness into the land of promise (3:6-11). The King described the Bride as though she was both the land of promise and the Garden of Eden (4:1-15), and then the relationship was consummated with divine approval (4:16–5:1).

Whereas the Bride had longed for the King before the wedding (Song 3:1-5), after the wedding she did not feel the same, refusing him when he came knocking in the night (5:2-8). The King left a blessing and went away (5:5-6), prompting the Bride to seek him and extol his virtues (5:9-16). She realized he had gone down to his garden (6:1-3), recalled what he had earlier said to her (6:4-10), and went to the garden to meet him

(6:11). The King, having made preparation for her coming, swept her up in his love as she returned to him (6:12-13).

So the couple have courted (Song 1:1–3:5), married (3:6–5:1), experienced marital conflict and separation (5:2–6:10), and chapter 7 portrays the reconciliation that began at the end of chapter 6 (6:11–7:12). The Bride has returned (6:11-13), and the King now praises her. He will begin with her feet and work up to her head in 7:1-5, and then in 7:6-9 he will articulate his intention to enjoy the fruit of his garden, his bride. In 7:10-13 she states her intention to give him that fruit.[1]

Song 7:1-5, Beautiful Head to Toe

Song 7:6-9, I Will Lay Hold

Song 7:10-13, I Will Give

Song 7:1-5: Beautiful Head to Toe

When the Bride refused the King in 5:3, he evidenced no resentment as he left myrrh on the lock (5:5). Nor did he leave the Bride in order to go and do something to spite her. He went down to his garden (6:2), where she knew she would find him (6:11). Song 6:12 indicated that the King had prepared for the Bride's coming, preparing to welcome her back with thoughtful enthusiasm.

As the King begins to speak in 7:1-5, we see no bitterness, no recrimination. He welcomes her back with words of love that continue to articulate to her what she means to him.

There was abundant food in the Garden of Eden (Gen. 1:29-30), and gold and precious stones were there (2:11-12). In 7:1-5 Solomon depicts the King speaking of the Bride in terms of precious stones, intoxicating drink, abundant food, animal life, and the cities of the land of promise (7:1-5). Thus, the King continues to address the Bride as though she is the Garden of Eden in the Land of Promise to him.

The King begins in Song 7:1 with the words 'How beautiful,' and the same phrase will mark a new departure in 7:6. Having

---

1. I am using the enumeration of the verses found in English translations. The verse numbers in Hebrew and English are different because what English translations enumerate as 6:13 is numbered 7:1 in Hebrew.

praised her feet in 7:1, he moves up to her thigh, with a term that seems to refer to the shape of her body from her hip to the middle of her leg, describing the curvature there. Likening this part of her to 'jewels,' however, 'the work of a master hand' (7:1), takes us beyond the physical appearance into spiritual significance. Yes, she is beautiful. Yes, the jewels are precious stones, carefully worked, and this speaks to the rarity of what the King describes. He speaks of her in terms of objects of great beauty, of rare material, carefully crafted, gained only at great cost, and in view of the other aspects of his description of the Bride here and throughout the Song, this description recalls the precious stones in Eden.

In Song 7:2 he moves up from her feet and thigh in verse 1 to her navel. It may be the case that there were different standards of beauty in Solomon's day, so that whereas today the ideal is a flat stomach, Solomon preferred a round one. That may be the case, but again there is more to this description than what meets the eye. So the goblet of mixed wine, like the rare jewels, speaks of the privileged enjoyment of delectable pleasures. The description may have nothing to do with her appearance and everything to do with the enjoyment of high delights of the richest fare. The same might be why her belly is likened to a heap of wheat in a field hedged with flowers. There could be a double entendre in the wheat encircled by lilies, the connotations of fine food and rich fare joining with the suggestive description of the appearance of her body, naked and without shame.

As he has done earlier in the Song (Song 4:5), the King again likens the Bride's chest to the tender, delicate young of a graceful, beautiful animal. And again, the point is not that her breasts look like the young of a gazelle but that she is tender, beautiful, and like the land of promise under the blessing of God sustaining new life. This description speaks to the enjoyment of fertility as a blessing of the covenant.

Familiar too, from what the King said before (Song 4:4; 6:4), in 7:4-5 he compares her to towers and cities. The tower signifies the protection of the Davidic King. The cities hint at the expanding of the boundaries of the land of promise. The King probably does not say the flowing locks of her hair 'are like purple' in 7:5 because she had purple hair but because of its symbolic value: purple being associated both with royalty and the tabernacle and temple. The end of verse 5 speaks of the King as captive in the tresses, pointing both to the way he is mesmerized by her beauty, and to the way that he must love her to bring about the fulfillment of God's purposes. These descriptions indicate that the King likens the Bride to the flourishing of God's purposes among God's people.

Why would the King speak of the Bride in these terms? It seems that the King understands that his marriage to this woman is a mini-drama of the covenant between Yahweh and Israel. The King seems to understand that his love for his Bride is to be like Yahweh's love for Israel: unfaltering, unimpeachable, and uninterrupted. The Lord will accomplish His purposes on earth. He will show His faithfulness. He will cause His glory to cover the dry lands like the waters cover the seas. And the King seems to understand that his relationship with the Bride is enacting Yahweh's faithfulness to Israel. The King uses the terms and categories of what matters most to him—God's blessing on the land in which the King exercises dominion as God's vice-regent—to describe the beauty of his Bride, who matters most to him.

Do you think of your marriage this way? Do you see it as an opportunity to enact the covenant between God and Israel, Christ and the church? Are you able to describe your beloved using terms that communicate God's blessing on your vocation?

Are you so committed to your spouse that it really doesn't matter how you are treated, because you are going to love your spouse the way that the Lord loves His people, the way His people should respond to Him? In view of the way the Bride rejected him in 5:3, that is the nature of the King's response here. He does not reprove his Bride. He does not correct her. He does not initiate a review of her mistakes. He goes straight to what matters: her significance to him as an emblem of the fulfillment of the promises of God and the redemption and renewal of all things.

Song 7:6-9: I Will Lay Hold
The King had started with the words 'How Beautiful' in 7:1, and now he repeats them in 7:6. The repetition marks a new

departure. The King has restated the Bride's significance to him in 7:1-5, and in 7:6-9 he communicates his intention to enjoy their renewed intimacy.

He extols her beauty and sweetness in 7:6, and then in 7:7-8 it may be that he means to recall an unpleasant memory from Israel's past, which he means to reverse. We are all too sadly familiar with distortions and perversions of the glory of what God has given, particularly distortions and perversions of marital bliss. Solomon's poetry here suggests a particular distortion in Israel's history, and as he alludes to the sad event the King in the Song puts the wrong right by laying positive connotations over the negative ones. It is as though the King overwrites a corrupt piece of software with renewed and correct code.

The poetic allusion in view here stems from the fact that the word rendered 'palm tree' in Song 7:7-8 is made of the same consonants and vowels as the name Tamar, a name familiar from Genesis 38 and 2 Samuel 13. In Genesis 38 Judah used his daughter-in-law Tamar as a prostitute, a gross perversion of God's intention for marital intimacy. In 2 Samuel 13 Amnon seized Tamar, his sister, and raped her (cf. 2 Sam. 13:11, 14), another twisted corruption of God's good gift. Neither prostitution nor rape should feature in the history of the people of God. These horrors would be associated with the name Tamar, and these wrongs will be set right in the Song. Here in Song 7:7-8, the King approaches a 'Tamar,' a palm tree, and he says that he is going to 'lay hold of its fruit' (Song 7:8). In this context, a context celebrating renewed intimacy in marriage, the King taking the fruit of his tree accomplishes the overwriting of the bad file. The King has conducted himself in honor and righteousness where Judah and Amnon were shameful and unrighteous.

In Song 7:7-8, the King also once again draws on terms and imagery used for the land of promise to describe the Bride. The 'clusters of the vine' (7:8) are reminiscent of the famous 'cluster of grapes' that the spies of the land brought back in Numbers 13:23. The King will enjoy the fruit the Israelites were too timid to take. Not only is the King approaching his 'Tamar' — the palm tree — in righteousness where Judah and Amnon used their Tamars in unrighteousness, the King's palm-tree-Bride willingly gives herself in 7:10-13, saying that she wishes he were 'like a brother' in 8:1. The Bride wishing the King were a beloved brother again engages the distorted brother-sister relations between Amnon and Tamar, overlaying negative connotations with positive.

Unfortunately, we all have a history like Israel's. Every one of us can point to things in our lives that never should have been part of our story, just as the nation of Israel could point to Genesis 38, Numbers 13, and 2 Samuel 13. Here in Song 7:7-8, Solomon the author depicts an idealized Solomon the King rewriting history by reliving it well, undoing the wrongs by setting them right, and this typifies the one who will come and re-live the history of Israel in righteousness.

Jesus was obedient where the nation of Israel transgressed. Jesus took responsibility for Israel's sin. He lived the righteous life they should have lived. He was put forward by the Father as a sacrifice of propitiation.

How are you going to deal with the parts of your story that are like Genesis 38 and 2 Samuel 13? What are you going to do about those dark secrets, those things you don't want anyone to know? If you will take these things to Jesus, if you will believe that by His death He paid the penalty, by His resurrection He conquered, you can be forgiven. Your corrupt files can be overwritten by the righteousness of Christ, and because of your faith in Jesus the Father will reckon you righteous.

Do you have a history of the corruption and perversion of God's good gift of marital intimacy? The Song of Solomon sings a song of hope for you. Bad connotations can be overwritten by positive action that lives out God's instructions for righteousness. You can change. The Lord Jesus can make the Tamars of your history into the palm trees of the Song of Solomon by the power of His Spirit at work as He sanctifies you by the Word of God.

The King in the Song typifies the hero, the only hero, the only one worthy of trust, worship, and obedience. The King in the Song typifies Jesus.

Song 7:10-13: I Will Give
Solomon's depiction of the King welcoming the Bride back with words of love in Song 7:1-9 movingly suggests that his

actions will right the wrongs of Israel's history. The Bride's words in Song 7:10 join the song of hope, as her lines point to the reversal of the oldest of curses.

The Bride opens in Song 7:10 with the words she spoke in 6:3, 'I am my beloved's,' a statement similar to 2:16, 'My beloved is mine, and I am his.' In 6:3 she said, 'I am my beloved's and my beloved is mine,' and now in 7:10 she says, 'I am my beloved's, and his desire is for me.' The term rendered 'desire' only occurs three times in the whole of the Hebrew Bible: Genesis 3:16; 4:7; and Song 7:10.

In Genesis 3:16 the word 'desire' appears in the curse that the woman's desire would be for her husband and he would rule over her. From Genesis 4:7, we see what this means. The Lord told Cain in Genesis 4:7 that sin's desire was for him but he must rule over it, the same terms seen in Genesis 3:16 appearing in 4:7. These passages are mutually interpretive. Sin's desire was to master Cain, to control him, to dictate his actions. That seems to be the nature of the desire the woman is cursed to have in 3:16. She was made to help the man (Gen. 2:18), but God's word of judgment against sin is that instead of wanting to help she will desire to control. Just as Cain needed to master sin by ruling over any sinful inclination, refusing to tolerate tempting impulses, the man would rule harshly over the woman.

Genesis 3:16 thus places a curse on the relations between man and woman, a curse that will have the woman wanting to control and the man responding with iron-fisted rule. The Bride speaks in Song 7:10 of the reversal of the Genesis 3:16 curse. She relinquishes the desire to rule with the words 'I am my beloved's,' and she places the 'desire' to lead where it belongs—in the heart of the husband—with the words 'and his desire is for me.'

Song of Songs 7:10 depicts the setting right of a relationship that has been distorted since the curse that came against the original sin. The reuse of this term 'desire' in Song 7:10, a term only ever used elsewhere in all the Bible in Genesis 3:16 and 4:7, indicates that the reconciliation depicted here will be *as far reaching as the curse has been*. All humanity was plunged into sin as a result of what Adam did (Rom. 5:12-21; 1 Cor. 15:21-22), and the curse on all humanity will be rolled back when the son of David makes things right with His Bride.

The words of the Bride in Song 7:10 point to an eschatological, end-time, latter-day expectation: a hope that when the King from David's line has made things right with His Bride, the curses of Genesis 3 will be rolled back and the way to Eden will be reopened.

> Let the mountains dance and the seas sing praise!
> Let the rivers clap and the clouds all break!
> Let the barren give birth and the prisoner go free!
> Let the serpent lie crushed, the earth rejoice, and all heaven sing:
> Jesus has overcome.
> Jesus conquered, bringing blessing that rolls back curses.
> Jesus is King.
> Worship Him.

There is shameless nakedness in the sentiments the Bride states from Song 7:11 through 8:4. The vineyards were in bloom when the King invited her to be his Bride in 2:13. The King entered that fertile vineyard and enjoyed all the 'choicest fruits' of his garden when the marriage was consummated in 4:16–5:1. The Bride's refusal jeopardized their relationship, and eventually she returned to see if the vines had budded in 6:11. Now she invites him in 7:11-12 to go out to see if the vines have budded, and of her own volition she declares, 'I will give you my love' (Song 7:12).

As she speaks of 'mandrakes' in Song 7:13, we read the reversal of yet another failure in Israel's past, the failure recounted when Leah bought Jacob from Rachel at the price of mandrakes (Genesis 30). All those past sins are gone, and the words that had unpleasant associations are being used to create good memories in place of the bad ones. She speaks of 'choice fruits,' too, in 7:13, and we last read about choice fruits at the consummation of the relationship in 4:16 (cf. also Song 4:13).

The choice fruits that the King gathered at the consummation of the wedding in 4:16–5:1 will be enjoyed anew in Song 7:13, as the Bride speaks of the 'new as well as old' delights that she has prepared for the King. The King has again spoken words that have freed the Bride. Because he did not accuse or condemn her after she refused him, because by leaving myrrh on the latch he conducted himself so that she would want to seek him, because he made preparation for her to be swept up in his chariots when she returned to him, because he spoke words of love to her that communicated her significance to him, and because he made plain his intention to renew the joy of their marital union, she gladly gives herself.

Husbands, love your wives as the King loves the Bride in the Song of Songs. Wives, nothing will be more exciting to your husbands than for you to speak the way the Bride does in Song 7:11-13. She is inviting, mysterious, promising, and prepared with choice fruits old and new. May God so bless our marriages.

Conclusion

Apart from the revelation of the curse in Genesis 3:16, we would not know what our problems are. Apart from the depiction of the reversal of the curse in Song 7:10, we might not hope that things once cursed could be made new by blessing. Apart from the way that Solomon depicts the King typifying Jesus, we might not have hoped that he would be so good. Apart from the conquest Jesus accomplished, we would have no hope that it could be done. Jesus has done it.

The unfolding drama of the Song of Songs parallels the story of Yahweh and Israel. The Sinai covenant was the marriage. Israel refused Yahweh, who exiled Israel from the land. He said that from exile, Israel would seek Him, as the Bride sought the King in the Song, and then just as the Bride returned to the King, Israel would repent and return to the Lord. At that point the great reconciliation, of which the renewal of marital intimacy in the Song is but a type and shadow, will be consummated. The curses will be rolled back. The praise will never end.

Questions for Discussion

1. This book operates from the perspective that the meaning and significance of the statements in Song

of Songs 7 go well beyond a literal, straightforward reading of the mere words of the poetry. Do you agree that poetry does function this way? Do you think that poetry uses terms that evoke meanings and significance well beyond the bare meaning of the statements a poem makes?

2. This study treats earlier Old Testament Scripture as the primary background of the poetry of the Song of Songs. Do you agree with this suggestion? If not, what other background would be more prominent for King Solomon?

3. This chapter has understood Solomon to be presenting significant reversals of the accounts of Tamar, brother-sister relations, the failure in Numbers 13, the Genesis 3:16 curse, and the incident with the mandrakes in Genesis 30. Do you agree that Solomon intended to evoke these events and present righteous re-enactments in the poetry of the Song?

4. In this chapter it was suggested that Solomon meant the King's righteous re-enactments to typify the expected redeemer from the line of David, the Christ. What do you think of this way of understanding the Song's poetry?

5. How does Song of Songs 7 influence the way you think about your life and relationships?

9

The Meaning and Application of the Song
(Song of Songs 8)

If you are married, is your experience of intimacy in marriage sullied with unpleasant memories or associations? If you are single, are you dreading intimacy in marriage because of unpleasant memories or associations? When you think of intimacy in marriage, are there awful things that have happened in your past, things that have been done to you that you did not want, that cloud the skies? Or are there selfish choices that you have made that turn blue skies black?

Perhaps you're not thinking of any one thing that's happened or any particular choice you made, perhaps you're afflicted with the simple knowledge that you're a sinner, that all your experiences are affected by your propensity to do wrong. Is there any hope? Is there any hope for fallen, sinful people who have been abused and maybe abused others? Is there any hope for us to enjoy the glories of what God intended when He created marital intimacy?

Song of Songs 8 is in the Bible to teach that the wrongs will be reversed and that human love derives its meaning and purpose from the character of God's love.

Our hope is in Jesus, the one who reverses wrongs, whose blessings overcome curses. Our hope is in having our thinking about marriage and intimacy within marriage renewed and transformed by the character of God's love. God's love is to be the paradigm and pattern for our love. God's love is to be the ground and impetus for our love. God's love gives meaning to human love, and human love exists to display God's love.

We can summarize the relationship that unfolds between the King and his Bride in the chapters of the Song of Songs as follows:

Song 1–3	Courtship
Song 3–4	Wedding
Song 5–6	Separation
Song 6–7	Reconciliation
Song 8	Resolution, Meaning, and Application

Song of Songs 8 falls into the following sections:

8:1-4	Resolution: Longing and Love
8:5-7	God's Love Gives Meaning to Ours: A Seal Stronger Than Death, A Flame Waters Won't Quench
8:8-10	Application to Singles: A Call for Purity
8:11-14	Application to Spouses: The Vineyard

Song 8:1-4: Longing and Love

Song of Songs 8:1 seems to indicate that the society in which this poem was composed is one that would frown on a wife doing things that a sister would be free to do. It seems that the Bride is saying that she wants the freedom to express her affection for her husband.

We noted when we looked at Song 7:7-8 that the word 'palm tree' in Hebrew is the same as the name Tamar. The use of the term Tamar provided a set of positive connotations for that word, replacing and overcoming the negative connotations of Genesis 38 and 2 Samuel 13. Then in Song 7:10 the language of Genesis 3:16 was reversed, with relationships between man and wife set right, and in Song 7:13 'mandrakes' are used in an appropriate way. The statement about the Bride wanting to be the King's sister in Song 8:1, with her adding that she would have them be not only children of the same father but of the same mother—nursing at the same breasts—replaces the negative connotations not only of 2 Samuel 13 with Amnon and Tamar, but also recalls the unfortunate sister-fibs told by Abraham and Isaac.

Here at the end of the Song of Songs, negative memories from Israel's past are re-scripted in a positive direction.

Even in the context of this reunion that has been underway since Song of Songs 6:11, the Bride longs for more. It's as though she is aware, as good as things are, that things could be better still. This longing for more is also seen in 8:2, where as in 3:4 she speaks of a desire to take the King into the house of her mother, and as in 4:16–5:1 she speaks of giving the King spiced wine and the juice of her pomegranate. The refusal of 5:3 has been replaced by a readiness that the Bride has been communicating since 7:9.

The longing for more that we feel should not be allowed to fester into a discontented, restless, idolatrous way of seeking to have our desires fulfilled in this world. The longing for more we feel tells us that as good as things may be in this world, we were made for a better covenant in a better place with a better mediator.

Could it be possible to have a relationship that miraculously conjoins all the best aspects of marital and sibling relations? Are you able to imagine what it will be like to see Jesus as He is, He who is both the Bridegroom and our elder brother? The longing the Bride articulates in Song of Songs 8:1-2 shows her yearning for a great marriage that partakes of all the best aspects of an appropriate brother-sister relationship. Her searching words grasp at the fulfillment of that to which both marriage and family point. She here communicates her longing for the consummation of the relationship between God and His people.

Note that in Song of Songs 8:2 Solomon has the Bride referencing the way she was taught by her mother. These relationships are appropriate. The Bride does not disobey her mother. Rather, she does what her mother taught her to do. She does not pursue forbidden, immoral relations, but sanctioned, endorsed relations with her husband. The fact that her mother taught her, puts us in mind of an older woman teaching the younger to love her husband, as Paul instructs older women to do in Titus 2.

What the Bride says in Song of Songs 8:3-4 is similar to what she said in 2:6-7 and 3:5 (cf. 5:8). In the impressionistic narrative that unfolds across the Song, the first two times she makes a statement like this she speaks as one who needs to heed her own words and not awaken love before her own marriage: in a courtship scene in 2:6-7, and just before the wedding in 3:5. Now she communicates her conviction to the unmarried as one who has experience with marriage.

Let me encourage you to apply the words of the Bride as follows: while we wait for the coming of the King, use your good relationships to fuel your longing for the coming of Jesus. If you have a great marriage, think how much better its fulfillment will be. If you love a brother or sister in your earthly family, think of what it will be to walk with Jesus, 'the firstborn among many brothers' (Rom. 8:29) in the family of God. Long for Him. Keep yourself pure for Him. Train those under your care to be pure for their earthly spouses and for the heavenly Bridegroom. He will come and make all things new. Wait for Him.

Song 8:5-7: God's Love Gives Meaning to Ours: A Seal Stronger Than Death, A Flame Waters Won't Quench

The question 'Who is that coming up from the wilderness?' in 3:6 introduced the coming of Solomon into Jerusalem for his wedding (cf. 3:11) in terms reminiscent of the way the Lord led Israel up from the wilderness into the land of promise. The point of the imagery was to identify Solomon with Yahweh Himself and the Bride with Israel. The consummation of the covenant-wedding was poetically depicted (4:1–5:1), followed by the Bride's rejection of the King (5:3), and his withdrawal (5:4-6). The Bride was disciplined by the watchmen (5:7), and then the Bride reflected on the King and sought him (5:8–6:11). The King swept her up in his love, and their reunion was initiated (6:12–8:4).

Now in Song of Songs 8:5 we encounter another instance of the question we saw in 3:6. The repetition of the question from 3:6 in 8:5 sets up another parallel with Israel's history. After the exodus from Egypt, Israel sojourned through the wilderness, and after the sojourn in the wilderness they conquered the land of promise. They then broke the covenant and were driven into exile. The prophets paralleled slavery in Egypt with exile to Babylon (e.g., Isa. 52:4; Hosea 11:5), and they indicated that when God saved Israel from exile, it would be according to the pattern of the exodus from Egypt but better (Isa. 11:16; Jer. 16:14-15). Israel's prophets taught that the Lord would again deliver Israel at a new exodus, that he would bring them back to the land, where they would enjoy a renewal of covenant with Him (Jer. 31:31-34; Hosea 2:14-23). The whole complex of events from the exodus through to the conquest would be repeated, and the repetition of the question from Song of Songs 3:6 in Song of Songs 8:5 points to a repetition of the exodus pattern.

Though Solomon lived before those prophets, his prayer in 1 Kings 8 at the dedication of the temple shows that he understood that Israel would be exiled from and brought back to the land. With the King in the Song corresponding to the Lord, and the Bride to Israel, the King's entrance into Jerusalem in 3:6-11 matches Yahweh's entrance into the land after the exodus. The Bride's rejection of the King is like Israel's rejection of the Lord, and now as the Bride comes up from the wilderness, leaning on her beloved in 8:5, it is as though there has been a new exodus, a new wilderness sojourn, and now there is a new entrance into the land. Understood this way, what we saw in Song of Songs 3:6 is repeated in 8:5 to point to the anticipated new covenant between the Lord and His people.

The drama between the King and the Bride in the Song of Songs points beyond itself to the drama being played out in world history between Yahweh and His people. The fact that it points beyond itself to something more important makes human love more meaningful, not less. That human love serves to display God's love makes the profound statements about human love in Song 8:6-7 better than they would be if they were constrained to the human level. These great statements are deepened by the fact that they draw their meaning from God's love for His people.

Thus, when Solomon depicts the Bride employing language and imagery reminiscent of earlier Scripture in Song of Songs 8:6-7, Yahweh's own love for His people provides the paradigm for the love between the King and the Bride. She speaks of a 'seal' on 'heart' and 'arm' in 8:6, echoing the way Israel was called to love Yahweh wholly in Deuteronomy 6:4-5, to have His words on their heart in 6:6 and as sign for hand and frontlet for forehead in 6:8. She speaks of love being strong as death in 8:6, bespeaking the love of the Lord that the curse of death cannot undo.

> Death promised to Adam if he ate of the tree.
> Death experienced when driven from Eden.
> Death promised to nation if they broke covenant.
> Death experienced when driven from land of life.
> Death known by the bones in that valley so dry.

Song of Songs 8:6 declares that 'Love is strong as death.' God's people incur the penalty of death because they sin, but God's love for them is as strong as their penalty and able to overcome it.

God's jealous love is 'fierce as the grave' (Song 8:6). It is God's holiness that will result in the death of His people. It is God's jealous concern for His own glory that will cause Him to visit the promised curse, the promised vengeance. God's love and God's jealousy: these are the paradigmatic expressions of love and jealousy. Every human expression of love or jealousy derives its meaning from God's love and jealousy. And our experience of death results from God's jealous commitment to His righteous truth.

To know God is to know these realities. This is what Song 8:6 means when it says, 'Its flashes are flashes of fire, the very flame of the LORD.' The 'its' in the phrase 'its flashes' refers back to jealousy, and jealousy truly communicated is an outworking of exclusive love. Flashes of jealousy, and by extension flashes of love, are 'the very flame of Yahweh.' Yahweh's love gives meaning to human love. Yahweh's relationship to Israel gives meaning to the King's relationship with his Bride. The King's relationship with his Bride can be known by every man and woman in marriage.

Song of Songs 8:7 goes on to declare, 'Many waters cannot quench love, neither can floods drown it.' Significant waters in Israel's history include the flood, the Red Sea, and the Jordan River, none of which stopped God's love for His people.

Yahweh's love is like 'flashes of fire,' and the waters won't quench it (Song 8:6-7).

The last words of Song 8:7 assert that people who think love can be bought do not understand it. Loyalty cannot be purchased. Fidelity has no price. No one can buy or sell genuine affection. No sum enables a buyer to acquire joy. These are gifts. They are gifts connected to the big truths of life.

We are loyal to our spouses because we want to show the truth about the love between God and His people. We are faithful because we know that God's way is right and want to live that, for Him and for ourselves. We show genuine affection because we feel the power of joy, the goodness of love; we know what it's like to have been loved, and we love like that in turn.

None of this is for sale. God's truth is not for sale. God's character cannot be constrained by cash. God is good. He is better than money. Money has no claim on Him. Money cannot buy salvation or love.

You want love? You need to know God. You need to see how He put Christ forward. He did not spare His own Son.

You want to have that love? It is free, without money and without cost. There is no price on it, but it will cost your whole heart, soul, mind, and strength.

Would you behold the supreme expression of love? Look to the cross.

Would you be loved this way? Trust Christ.

Would you show this love to others? Lay your life down for them as He did for you.

Solomon's desire for his audience to experience God's love results in the meditation that follows in 8:8-14, which is an application of the Song's message. Song of Songs 8:8-10 applies the Song to singles, and 8:11-14 applies it to spouses.

Song 8:8-10: A Call for Purity
In Song of Songs 8:8-10 Solomon teaches that on the one hand those who are pure will be rewarded and made more attractive, making them even more desirable; while on the other hand, those not wise enough to maintain purity should be helped to purity by those who care for them.

Do you recognize and value the glory of purity? Do you really? Are you helping others to value purity?

Or are you of two minds on purity? Are you the type who wants purity in your own spouse, but until you're married you don't mind using people for your own enjoyment, without regard for their defilement. Do you value the purity of the spouse you hope to have, while failing to value your own purity or the purity of others you won't marry?

Or, perhaps you value purity in actuality but not in your imagination? Have you applied your love for purity to what you let yourself think about?

Can you apply your love for purity to men or women who are being flounced before you as enticements to sin?

Can you apply your love for purity to those whose defilement is displayed in pictures and videos? Does their defilement make you weep for them? Do you recognize that they are being dehumanized, that something is being taken from them in exchange for money? Do you see how they are being used? That's what porn is. Porn uses people for money.

> Porn sells the purity of those who give away
> what they cannot get back
> so that they can have a little cash
> because in this warped and twisted world
> people are attracted to the display of the defiling of people.

Do you celebrate the purity of the pure? Do you seek to stymie the defilement of those not pure? That's what we're called to by this poetry, because that's what this Song calls for.

This Song shows how human love is derived from and displays God's love. That demands purity because God's love is pure. Therefore, we want to apply our experience of God's love, we want to celebrate purity and promote it, and we want to help those who don't understand the value of purity to experience its glory—for their own good, for the good of the spouse we hope they have, and for the glory of God to be shown forth in their lives.

The pure are rewarded. Song 8:10 shows the Bride saying that she was pure, she was celebrated, and this made her Solomon-like. There is a correspondence between Solomon's name and the Hebrew rendered 'one who finds peace'

(Song 8:10). By maintaining her own purity, the Bride made herself appropriate for King Solomon.

In the old covenant, those who are pure are like Yahweh. In the new covenant, those who are pure are like Christ.

Song 8:11-14: The Vineyard

The sentiments in Song of Songs 8:11-12 assume an understanding of the economy of Solomon's society.

> Solomon had a vineyard at Baal-hamon;
> he let out the vineyard to keepers;
> each one was to bring for its fruit a thousand pieces of silver.
> My own vineyard, my very own, is before me;
> you, O Solomon, may have the thousand,
> and the keepers of the fruit two hundred.

Verses 11-12 are likely informed by the understanding that the keepers of the vineyard were each to bring 1,000 pieces of silver produced by the fruit of the vineyard as the revenue for the use of the land. Solomon owns the land, and the keepers bring a thousand pieces of silver for the use of the land, for the ability to farm it and benefit from its fruit. The keepers' own share seems to be reflected in the statement that they can keep 200 pieces in 8:12. So this agreement between the keepers of the vineyard seems to be assumed, informing the Bride's statement in 8:12 that she is giving her vineyard entirely up to the King, to the idealized Solomon portrayed in the Song.

What does this mean? Married wives, this is an application for you. The picture of the Bride yielding herself to the King stands here at the conclusion of the Song.

Married husbands, your application is modeled by the King in 8:13. The King says to the Bride, 'O you who dwell in the gardens, with your companions listening for your voice; let me hear it.' He has identified her as a garden in chapter 4, and now she has identified herself as a vineyard in 8:12. In 8:13 the King seeks the joy of his beloved. She yields her vineyard to him in 8:12, and he asks to hear her voice in 8:13.

She provides what he wants, and he provides what she wants. She provides her vineyard for the King's enjoyment. He tells her he wants to hear her voice. A mutual understanding of the desires of the other is reflected in these statements at the end of the Song: mutual desire to please the other; mutual eagerness to enjoy what delights the other.

Solomon puts the last words of the Song on the lips of the Bride, and these last words are words she has said before, in 2:17. There are slight changes here, but she again invites the King to delight himself in his garden.

Conclusion

The Song depicts human love for us as the poetry presents an impressionistic love story that unfolds between an idealized portrait of the anointed King from the line of David and his perfect Bride. The love between the King and his Bride corresponds to the love between God and His people, and this correspondence is the ground for and the ultimate meaning of the human love it is our privilege to enjoy.

> Our hope is in Jesus, who reverses wrongs, whose blessings overcome curses.
>
> Our hope is in having our thinking about marriage and intimacy within marriage renewed and transformed by the character of God's love.
>
> God's love is the paradigm and pattern for our love.
>
> God's love is the ground and impetus for our love.
>
> God's love gives meaning to human love, and human love exists to display God's love.

Male students of the Song, be inspired to emulate the King, who himself typifies the Christ we are to follow. Female students of the Song, strive to be like the Bride, who typifies the church, redeemed by and submitting to the Lord Christ.

These glories will be fulfilled when Christ returns for the marriage feast of the Lamb (Rev. 19:7).

QUESTIONS FOR DISCUSSION

1. Song 8:6 says that jealousy's flashes are the flame of Yahweh. How does this statement inform the meaning of love and righteous jealousy?

2. Song 8:6 also says that love is strong as death. This chapter took that to mean that God's love will

overcome the curse of death. What else might this statement mean in the context of Song 8:6?

3. Song 8:7 speaks of the scorn that meets those who try to purchase love. If love cannot be bought, how is it to be gained?

4. When Song 8:9 says that if a young girl is a door she will be enclosed with boards of cedar, it means that if a young lady lets people in, her freedom to do that will be stopped. Are there ways this needs to be applied in your life? Are you committed to boarding up those who let people in where they should keep people out?

5. What section of the Song of Songs has most impacted you?

6. Has your love for Christ been stirred up through this study?

7. Are there action steps you should begin to take in response to what you have learned?

Subject Index

Scripture Index